Keep On Leading

Cover Art by Alexandre Rito www.designbookcover.pt

ISBN: 9781672555227

To my Abuelo, Papi Tuto and his advice before I left for combat:

"Ojos de Aguila, Paso de Elefante, y desconfianza hasta del viento."
-Rafael Reyes

Table of Contents

Maps

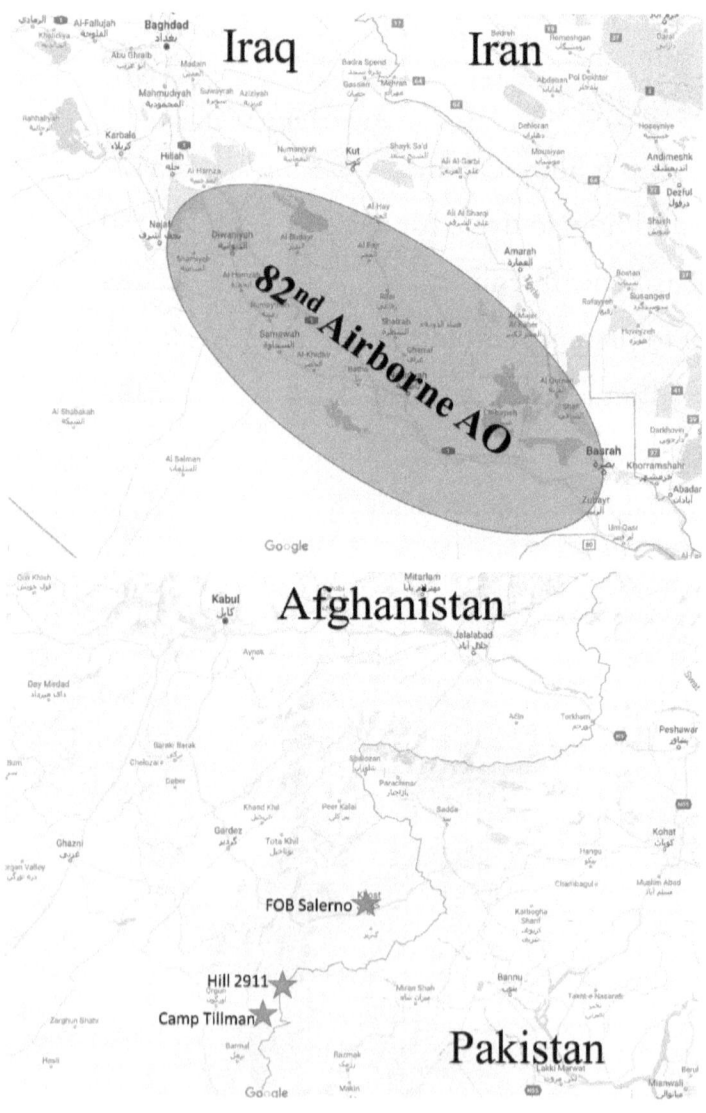

Forward

By Colonel Brandon Teague, Infantry, Commanding

Being a leader is one of the most professionally rewarding things that a person can do in business or the military, but it can also be one of the most frustrating if gone about in a way that is detrimental the organization. I have been a professional leader for almost 30 years in the U.S. military and have been in numerous situations that call for a brand of leadership that most read about in history books. When lives are on the line, you must be the best version of yourself as the consequences for failure are potentially catastrophic.

Being a leader is all about taking care of those that are in your charge whether that is in the military, business, school teacher, first responders or just your family; we all have an obligation to be a leader at some point in our lives. The one thing that has always brought me through the hardest of leadership situations is knowing that I am being counted by those around me to take care of them; we owe our subordinates nothing less. Being a leader is by no means easy. It takes a certain dedication to being better than others, both in your professional and in your personal life, as they all intertwine and will set the stage for success for you, your subordinates, and your organization.

In this book, Louis takes you through many different scenarios both during his time in the military and in business and gives you simple ideas and techniques to become the best version of leader that you can be. Some of these thoughts and techniques sound simple in principle but are extremely difficult in execution. Being a leader is sometimes knowing when to be a follower and letting the situation dictate what is needed. Everyone has a choice when it comes to leadership. You can be the leader that counsels your subordinates and displays what right looks like through your actions and not your words, or you can lead by fear. One style will motivate those around you to step up and do what is right and the other will have your subordinates doing what is required just to get by. No organization has ever achieved full success when the leader uses fear as a motivator; there are numerous cases throughout history that we can turn to that confirm this.

Subordinates just respond better when they are motivated by the leader in the organization. I have many times been asked why I have followed a certain leader that I found inspiring. The answer is quite simple; I didn't want to let them down. That is what inspiring leaders bring to the table. Through their actions, humility and empathy towards those that they lead, they inspire everyone to be the best version of themselves. That version is usually something that would be disappointed if anything less than success is achieved for the greater good of the organization. Do you respond well when you are berated in front of your peers when things did not go just right? How about being belittled because your work was not up to the standard that your boss thought was appropriate? These are the techniques of leaders who do not know how to lead and are trying to make up for their shortcomings. In this book Louis is trying to pass on some of those time-tested techniques of great leadership and make you and your organization more successful.

As you read this book, ask yourself what you would do in each one of these situations. Hopefully you have someone that you can turn too as a mentor to ask for guidance along the way. I self-reflect almost on a daily basis to ensure that I am doing the best that I can for those that I lead. I take the time in the morning to think about my day and put positive energy into being the best version of myself. As you read this book, think about that. What have you done today to make yourself, your organization and those around you better? Enjoy the book.

Introduction

Afghanistan, 2005

"Can I shoot?" We were patrolling mountains along the Afghanistan/Pakistan border when we stumbled on several men in military type gear moving in a patrolling formation. For a moment, we had the advantage. We had seen them and they still hadn't seen us. Silence was of the utmost importance. With hand and arm signals, those of us in front began relaying orders to the rest of the squad. I started to put my men into a hasty ambush position. As I began to give the order, the local interpreter that was with us pulled the charging handle on his AK-47 rifle and released it, making a loud metal clank.

Being at nearly 10,000 feet elevation on a remote Afghan mountain, there aren't very many sounds period, but the distinct clatter of a round being racked on a weapon can be heard for hundreds of yards. I stopped my hand signals and looked down at the sound. The interpreter looked up at me, his eyes filled with fear. I spun towards the enemy fighters who had clearly been alerted of our position. Time slowed down to a crawl. The enemy spotted our position, one of them turned his body towards us and lifted his weapon. That's when my squad leader asked the question, "Can I shoot?"

As the leader it was my job to know the rules of engagement. I had a fraction of a second to assess the situation and decide whether we were looking a friendlies, civilians, or enemy. I was quickly able to eliminate the possibility that they were civilian. Although there were local farmers in the area, they never walked in a formation, and these guys had extra magazine pouches on their chest. Local farmers and shepherds didn't carry extra magazines.

Now I had to decide whether they were Pakistani military, or Taliban fighters. The mismatched uniforms were a pretty good indicator that they were not Pakistani military, but that wasn't a guarantee. The kicker was that only the day before, we had been attacked by an enemy force in this area, and these guys looked just like them. Also, within a second of spotting us they had raised their weapons and were maneuvering for a fight.

"Shoot!" The round cracked out of my squad leader's weapon and hit the enemy fighter right in the head. A pink mist appeared behind his skull, his hands flew outwards and he fell to the ground. A second shot rang out, hitting another one of the enemies in formation in his side. He dropped his weapon, grabbed his side, then fell in a heap next to the first guy. One word, two dead, only a few seconds have passed.

Then the world around us erupted with bullets. Scores of rounds were zinging past, kicking up rocks, and splintering the few trees around us. I realized quickly that we had only seen a small portion of a much larger force, and based on the multiple directions the bullets were coming from, I could tell they were maneuvering around us.

"Bound back in fire teams!" I gave a quick order to my squad leader then grabbed the radio to call for artillery fire. We were on the side of the mountain with limited cover and poor visibility. We needed to move to higher ground where the terrain would allow for some natural protection and I could keep the enemy in front of us instead of all around us. The squad leader took over the movement of troops as I attempted radio contact. We were so high that I could see the base about 5 miles away as the crow flies. After my initial call that we were "troops in contact" (meaning in a firefight), no other communications were going through.

The volume of fire continued to increase. Now enemy grenades were being thrown at our position. To add to the difficulty, we were exhausted physically. We had only been in country a few weeks and were not accustomed to the thin air at these altitudes. We also carried 60 or more pounds between our body armor and ammunition. For the first few minutes of the fight, we moved rapidly and positioned ourselves, but we quickly got tired. I could barely speak as I gasped for air. It felt like I had just run a sprint at top speed, but now the situation required me to keep that pace for over an hour. I remember telling my legs to run in my head, but I could only walk as rounds zipped past me. My legs burned, and I felt like I was underwater. No matter how deep a breath I took, my lungs didn't seem to fill with oxygen.

"WHERE'S THE ARTILLERY?" My squad leader turned around yelling at the top of his lungs as I stood there with the radio handset to my ear attempting to communicate. "I'VE GOT NOTHING! Break contact, back to the trucks!" The radio was our lifeline, and the most powerful weapon we carried. With it, we could rain down so much firepower that even 100 enemy could not withstand. Right now, however, we were alone. Nine men, fighting an element three times our size with only our rifles and our training to rely on. In one of our vehicles we had a power amp and a heavy antenna which we could connect our radio to and guarantee communication. Our only chance at this point was to fight our way back to that lifeline.

"MEDIC!" The call came out, someone was hit. I stood up and looked in the direction of the scream. "HE'S AMBULATORY!" I now had an injury, but the call of "ambulatory" told me that he could walk. "Move him back, fast!" I gave the order and then turned to my radio operator. He couldn't even speak and was sitting against a tree simply trying to catch his breath. I knelt down so I was right in his face, "I want you to go all the way back to the trucks. Don't look back, don't wait for us. Don't stop until you get there. We will stay in between you and the enemy. Put this radio on the power amp and call fire on this position right here." I pointed down to the ground in front of him. His eyes got big and I could feel the protest in them. He wasn't about to call artillery on us. "We won't be here by then, the enemy will. Now go!" I grabbed his shoulders and helped him up, then sent him off the trail back towards the trucks.

I stood up straight, trying to get a better eye on the guy who was hurt, when I noticed some motion to my left. I spun around and saw an enemy fighter on our flank. He had climbed the mountain and popped up over the ridge. He had plunging fire on 5 of my men who were shooting at the bulk of the enemy force to our front. I could see the look on his face, he knew they hadn't noticed him. I quickly raised my weapon and fired a round in his direction. It hit the dirt in front of him, causing him to flinch. He spotted me, but before he could turn his weapon in my direction, I was already firing rounds two and three. He took off running and I continued to fire. The rounds were pinging off the ground all around him as I continued to make small adjustments; firing accurately under high stress from a standing position at a moving target 30 yards away is insanely difficult. Finally, he dropped back behind the ridge line and I did not see him again.

At that moment a round zinged towards me from my front, smacking the tree I was next to and flinging bark onto my cheek. The sting on my face had me worried. I touched my palm to my face and checked it for blood. As I looked down at my palm which was clear of blood, another round zinged by; this time coming from my right. At that instant, it was a like a loud voice in my head was yelling, "get down!" I dropped down and became one with the ground. I thought I spotted muzzle flashes coming from a bush in front of me and another to my right. I fired a magazine into each enemy position; 60 rounds in only a few seconds. The firing stopped.

I stood up quickly and took command of the battle again. Together, my squad leader and I moved the teams back up the trail. One team would fire and keep the heads of the enemy down while the other would move, then we would switch off again. We moved to a point where the natural disposition of the mountain prevented the enemy from flanking us. If they wanted to continue their attack, they would have to come straight on.

I had a brief conversation with my squad leader. At this point I was delegating the task of maneuvering the squad safely back to the trucks to him. I was going to go on ahead, get the radio up and running, and start getting artillery and air support in our direction. It had been over 45 minutes since our last radio communication.

I took off back to the trucks, made communication, informed the commander of our status, and got air support on the way. By the time the squad showed up, they were completely out of ammunition. The injured soldier had been shot in the face, but he was still shooting, moving, and smiling to let me know he was ok (we later found out the bullet went through his cheek and missed all teeth and bones). All of us were winded. It felt like I was trying to run and hold my breath at the same time. My unit was in no position to keep fighting, or to launch a counter attack. I was left with no other choice but to leave the battlefield.

It was a difficult day, and although we brought everyone home, I have always struggled with the decision to leave the battlefield. This is leadership. Some of you might be chasing a paycheck, looking for leadership opportunities, but I can tell you that every leader out has at least one decision they wish they never had to make; military or civilian.

Leadership is lonely, it's exhausting, and burdensome on your mind. If done right, however, it can be an immensely rewarding experience where you have the opportunity to effect real and positive change in organizations and people. You can leave a lasting mark on this world and do some real good. It's worth it to get it right.

This book is divided into three parts. They are arranged in a particular order, and the reader is strongly encouraged to internalize the book in the manner in which it was written. Take some time for self-reflection, identify the lessons that you can learn, and actually apply them with the mindset that is outlined.

I believe leadership is a skill, much like athleticism. Some are more suited to the task than others. Some are naturals, they exhibit the traits of outstanding leadership with little to no training and effort. These people, with some coaching, can become extreme change agents inside of your organization (either positive or negative). You may or may not fall into this category. If you do, this book will help you identify expressly some of the things you do that contribute to that skill and how to hone them. If you are not of the natural leadership variety, all is not lost. I believe that in these pages you will find the tips and motivation to learn and excel at the trade.

This book is set apart because it not only addresses the necessary areas of self-reflection required to be successful, but it also tells you how to examine the members of your team, and finally how to address the team as a whole. The most important part of this is that it reflects real-life experiences. This isn't a self-help book constructed out of the mind of theory in the realm of make-believe, it's based off of years of military and business experience, littered with mistakes made, and sprinkled with a dash of fun. I have had the distinct privilege of leading warriors on the battlefield, hardworking blue-collar employees, union members, and white-collar intellectuals. In every environment, I have been able to apply the leadership lessons outlined in this book to great success.

This book is divided into three distinct parts. The first section is **keep on leading yourself**. Instill self-discipline, have the right mental state, conduct yourself professionally, get your life in order, and more. The manager who is personally in debt, can't show up to work on time, looks unkempt, and can't keep his personal relationships out of the limelight and in order, is not likely to inspire his team. Being subject to addiction like alcohol, or obesity, or gossip will lower your standing in the group and prevent you from achieving your full potential.

The next section is **keep on leading people**. In this section you will be challenged to look at your team as individuals, each with different desires, needs, wants, goals, etc. You will be given tips on how to identify and harness the strengths of each player and what to do about those weaknesses everyone wants to focus on. I will teach you how to recognize your employees and also how to discipline them and have hard conversations. You will learn how to motivate them and encourage their creativity.

The final section, and the one most leadership books focus on is **keep on leading teams**. Here we will discuss setting goals and achieving them. How to properly challenge your team and how to build team cohesion. I will give you ideas and tips on how to communicate with the team to maximize results, get your message across, and get buy-in from the team. You will learn the secrets to getting more resources from those above you and how to create a team that is completely unstoppable.

So off you go now, enjoy the stories presented in the following pages. Try and find parallels in your own life. Internalize the lessons that are presented and apply them. Don't let the time spent reading this book be a waste. Also, set yourself a goal to actually finish this book. Don't let this become another half-read, dust covered, accessory on a shelf. You purchased this for a reason, or someone gave it to you because they felt you needed to read it. Keep that in mind and stay motivated to consume the content!

KEEP ON LEADING YOURSELF

1. Humility

Fort Bragg, 2005

I received a call from a personnel officer not long after my graduation from Airborne school. The unit I was going to had been informed that I had graduated and wanted to know where I was and how long before I would be at Fort Bragg. I was a single 22-year-old Lieutenant, eager to finally start my career, so I told him I'd be there in less than 8 hours and drove straight through.

I arrived at the headquarters, still wearing the comfortable jeans I had changed into for my drive. Generally, it's not advised to meet your new Colonel in civilian clothes, but I thought I'd get some "brownie points" for driving across several states to get there. The crisp February air filled my lungs as the sun was starting to set and my Army career was about to take off. The nerves filled my stomach as I walked into the headquarters building for the first time.

A young soldier at the front desk directed me to the colonel's office upstairs. I was greeted by the personnel officer that had spoken to me on the phone that morning. The building was mostly empty as it was late on a Friday afternoon, but I could still see the man in charge (or his silhouette) at his desk plugging away. "He's expecting you," the senior Lieutenant motioned towards the colonel's door. I knocked, "Lieutentant Fernandez reporting as ordered sir." He looked up from his computer, "Report."

I stepped into the office and stood with my body rigid, back straight, chest out, thumbs along the seams of my pants at attention. He was a rather large man with short grey hair. He stood up and looked to be over six feet and 230-240lbs with a presence about him. Although I hadn't been in the Army very long, I was still familiar with the badges on his uniform: Ranger, Jumpmaster, Combat Infantryman.

"Tell me Lieutenant, did you earn your tab?"

I expected the question. My close friend, who had joined the same unit a month before me told me about another LT that showed up to the 82nd Airborne without his Ranger Tab. My friend excitedly told me the story, "Dude, I walked in and that was all they wanted to know. Then there was this other guy who didn't have his…I think he got hurt or something…and he want to Bravo, which is where I think you're going to go, but that company commander was pissed that he was getting an LT without a Ranger tab. Just be ready for it!"

"Yes sir," I responded and a smile came over my face. Graduating Ranger school still sits at one of the peak accomplishments in my life. I walked out of there believing that I was invincible. I don't mean in some figurative "I was on top of the world sense", but in the very literal, "I can conquer anything, I'm invincible" sense. I already, as a part of my personality, toe the line between confidence and arrogance. The worst thing for that cocky 22 year old was to believe, TRULY believe, that there was nothing that could defeat him.

"Good," his demeanor relaxed and he let out his breath, "You'll be going to Bravo company." My friend was right. I smiled again as the colonel grabbed the phone and called my new boss to his office. He hung up the phone and finally invited me to sit down. For the next few minutes we had an informal interview with the standard, where are you from, why did you want to come to the 82nd, interview/chit-chat questions before Captain Teague knocked on the office door.

The first time I laid eyes upon the man that would change my life forever, he didn't look like much. Teague, unlike our commander, wasn't particularly tall, he didn't have a lot of muscles, and had a quiet demeanor. His smile was kind and gentle, and his handshake was strong but not overpowering. We all three exchanged some niceties and Teague whisked me away to the company headquarters to see where I would be working.

As we walked, he told me a bit about the platoon I was going to be taking over. Apparently they had had a string of bad leaders, so while the shoes I had to fill weren't very big, I would have a serious challenge winning the men over. They had grown a distaste and disrespect towards new Lieutenants (understandably so), and the Platoon Sergeant had been holding it all together. "Staff Sergeant Anderson is a very strong leader and a big personality, it would be wise of you to listen to him and remember it's his platoon."

We sat down in his office and continued our chat. He started to outline his leadership principles, but I was distracted. Sitting in his office was my first glimpse at who this man in front of me actually was. He had a large plaque from the best ranger competition, which is a competition of the most skilled Army rangers, and few of them even complete the multi-day gauntlet of events. Teague was not only selected and finished the competition, but it looked as though he had a trophy of some sort.

"There's a platoon live fire on Monday, you're going to lead your platoon. The XO will give you some gear." In a rush I was snapped back to reality. I still hadn't met my platoon, let alone even unpacked my car and they were already giving me gear to lead them in a live ammunition event in 48 hours, oh, and we were deploying to Afghanistan in less than 2 months.

The next few weeks were difficult and humbling. I got to know my men, lead them in a simulated combat exercise, and learn about the leadership challenges they had faced before I got there.

Here was my very first lesson in leadership: shut your damn mouth, you don't know anything yet! This lesson is one I have implemented everywhere I have started a new position. Captain Teague told me to be quiet and learn from my Platoon Sergeant, but the bigger lesson was to never enter a new place and start making changes immediately.

After a week in the woods playing army with my new set of 35 friends, we came back to the base to start preparations for deployment. I finally got a chance to unpack my bags, find a house, and get issued some gear. Then before we left, Captain Teague took all his officers on a run…

The name of the hill was Coolyconch. When spoken I could see the faces of my fellow Lieutenants writhe in pain before we even began to step off. It was a six-mile run: a little over three miles uphill to the top of Mt. Coolyconch, and 3 miles back.

It was brutal.

It was embarrassing.

I couldn't keep up.

As soon as we hit the hill, I started to fall back. I distinctly remember seeing my fellow officers up ahead on this red dirt trail jumping like gazelle's up the mountain, seemingly unchallenged. Meanwhile, I was fighting just to keep air in my lungs and liquid in my stomach. They waited for me at the top, a stern look of disappointment on Teague's face when I finally reached the summit, and the run continued.

We got to the end and Teague sat me down immediately to counsel me on his expectations of me as a leader. You see, we didn't do much actual running in Ranger school, then in Airborne school, our runs were pretty slow and short. I had basically been coasting along, living inside the arrogance in my head that I was some sort of big bad Ranger and I didn't need to train my body anymore. I had grown to believe that somehow, my previous successes were enough, that I could live in the past as if thousands of other people hadn't accomplished the same feat too. I couldn't earn the respect of my men with a Ranger tab, I had to earn it by being the leader they deserved. That small piece of cloth on my shoulder wasn't going to magically repel the enemy, and if I wasn't fit enough to handle extreme activity in arduous terrain, men's lives were at risk.

My arrogance was going to get someone killed. Luckily it wasn't so thick that I didn't learn this lesson that morning:

What you have done has gotten you where you are, but it won't take you where you're going.

I can rant and rave about all the things I've accomplished in the past, but none of them accomplish anything in the future. I had to learn that lesson in humility and stop trying to thrust my previous accomplishments into the present as some sort of qualifier for whatever task was at hand. Whatever you have accomplished, no matter how great, has absolutely no bearing on what you are about to do.

Understand there is a place for your laurels. They fill your own ego and give you the confidence to tackle the next task. They provide a good basis for you to have some lessons learned, some previous mistakes made, some pitfalls to avoid in the future. They may even illicit a small measure of respect from those around you, but without action of the same magnitude, your previous accomplishments mean nothing.

I assume if you're reading this, you want to be a great leader. You want to be respected, you want your opinions to matter, and you want your teams to do great things. If so, you must never rely on your past to give you credit in the future, and you must learn to be humble.

I want you to take a moment and think about people you've known in the past. I want you to think about those that were always quick to brag about something they had accomplished. These folks are the notorious "one-uppers", the type that always has to one-up your story and tell you why they are better, or what they did was better, or at least that they're just as good as you. Now let me ask you, did those people ever inspire you? Did they ever make you want to follow them? Did they make you want to do your best work? Probably not.

In the US Army, the Special Forces, or Green Berets, are known as the "quiet professionals." You see, when you have accomplished something real, when you have challenged yourself and actually made it, you don't need to spend a lot of time talking about how badass you are. You can be confident without being arrogant, and best of all, you can be humble.

When I think back to Captain Teague, I am reminded about the strength he had in his humility. That man never once, in the two years I worked for him, needed to talk about himself. Meanwhile, he could run most of the company into the ground, he was a tactical mastermind, bold and courageous in the face of overwhelming odds (even earning a silver star on our deployment to Afghanistan), and to this day one of the greatest leaders I have ever met. I'm sure you've heard the saying, "I'd follow that man straight to hell" often sputtered with a tinge of honesty, but I can tell you without a doubt, I would follow that man to victory in hell itself. Teague once asked me to assault a mountaintop against a fortified enemy that was five times bigger than my force, and I did it…with a smile.

This is the power of great leadership, this is the power that I learned over 15 years of leading men. Under great leadership, people will surprise you with what they can accomplish. They will astonish you with the extremes they will push themselves. They will shock you with how creative they become. They will further humble you with the loyalty they portray. They will overwhelm you with pride by their teamwork.

Humility, however, needs to be genuine. Don't self-deprecate in an attempt to feign humility. The other fake attempt at humility is the humble-brag, which is often a quick step behind the self-deprecating falsity. You can take a moment and conduct a quick internet search and find examples of people saying things like, "I look 'terrible' without makeup" or "I'm so humbled to have a job good enough to afford this amazing car/house/whatever". The attempt at humility is so obviously disingenuous that it serves the opposite from the desired effect and turns people completely off.

For an example on humility, I'd like to take you back a couple thousand years to a Jewish Carpenter in the Middle East. Regardless your feelings about the veracity of Christ's supernatural claims, his example of leadership is certainly one worth paying attention to and has lessons for the secular as well as the religious.

In the book of John chapter 13, it was the night of the Passover meal, and the night where Jesus would give his final lessons before his crucifixion. Without prompting, saying nothing, Jesus gets up, takes off his robe, wraps a towel around his waist, and begins to wash the feet of his disciples. Peter, who would later become one of the leaders of the Christian church, objects to his teacher putting himself in such a lowly position, "No you shall never wash my feet."

The Bible doesn't spend much time on this simple interaction, but it's important to note the type of humility Jesus uses as an example. You see, Jesus never calls himself humble, instead he humbles himself. He does the job of the lowest servant with Joy because it needed done. He never self-deprecates, he doesn't pretend to not have power, he doesn't "humble-brag", he doesn't talk about how humble he is. No, instead he dresses himself down, and through his actions, shows his humility. He proves that he is willing to do any job, that nothing is below his stature and place, and all people have worth.

This is an incredibly powerful tool that can set you apart as a leader very quickly. I learned this lesson early in my military career, not long after the Coolyconch run when I realized I had much to learn and started carefully observing the great leaders around me. Those that commanded the most respect made sure that every one of their soldiers had a chance to eat before they got in the line for food. They were the first to pick up a broom when cleaning needed done. They slept in the trenches with their men, in the same conditions. They took the midnight guard shift. They proved their humility through their actions, and their men absolutely adored them for it.

I quickly realized what a powerful force humility through action was and started to implement it immediately in my own leadership. Throughout my career I have used this tool and changed my mindset. I now make sure to place myself last and place the needs of my employees before my own. If I look back at my career at the single biggest contributor to my success as a leader, it has been through having a genuine servant leader outlook.

All of this is in your hands. You have the power to be a great leader and create amazing teams. You can do this tomorrow and immediately you will see changes. Place yourself last, and your team will respond in ways you cannot expect. They will sacrifice more, push themselves further, become more creative, and the list goes on. It starts by finding your humility and leading yourself!

TAKE ACTION:

What is one thing you can do with your team to humble yourself? Maybe you can pick up a broom and sweep up or help someone with a difficult task. Whatever it is, find some way you can humble yourself this week and do it. Go on, pick up your phone that's nearby and set a reminder right now.

2. The Winningest Attitude

North Carolina, 2015

"The morale of the team you're taking over is very low."

I have heard these words again and again. I'm not sure if my boss was telling me because she expected that I could change it, or to manage my expectations. I had billed myself as a go-getter, always willing to take on additional challenges, find creative solutions to problems, and never let "no" stop me during my interview. Now she was giving me the job of taking over a team whose product had been on the shelf for years, never making it to the marketplace.

My job was a program manager at one of the largest companies in the world, John Deere. The program manager is tasked with managing the entire product life cycle, from working with marketing to identify market opportunities, to developing technologies, to building a business case, managing a budget, directing the design, staying on top of the testing, building the assembly line, and helping with "go to market" activities. It's a critical role, but I was given a throwaway project.

I spent a lot of time observing the team in meetings and seeing how they approached work. Most felt like they were on a treadmill going nowhere. This product was never going to go to market, and all their efforts were effectively a waste of time. They had spent THREE years in the preliminary phases of the project. They had gone to the director multiple times to attempt to get funding for the project, and every time the decision was kicked down the road. It had become a big joke that project Thunder as it was aptly named, made a bunch of noise, but never accomplished anything in the physical realm.

I arrived fresh off a victory at a previous factory where I led a team to design a product, build it, test it, and bring it to market in less than eight months and for under a quarter million dollars. At a company this size, that is absolutely unheard of. Bringing something to market in under 3 years and for less than $5 million is basically a miracle; I know half the people I told the story to didn't believe me.

A typical program at this company has six phases:
1. Business Plan
2. Project Definition
3. Product Development
4. Project Demonstration
5. Project Implementation
6. Continuous Improvement

For those of you familiar with the Military Decision Making Process (MDMP), you'll see some parallels. This particular project had never made it out of Phase 2.

Imagine for three years they had built a business plan, defined a scope, developed a schedule, built prototypes, then got denied project funding and asked to go back to business plan. Again and again, this team had been on this Ferris wheel, slowly murdering their morale until the horse was fully dead.

Through their bad attitude, as a result of never getting the program approved, many of the team members had developed a perception of poor performance. In addition, the under-performing employees of several functional areas were quickly shuffled onto this team as a place to hide them. The best members of the team were only there as an additional duty, it wasn't their primary role.

I arrived full of energy and excited to take on this challenge. My boss told me the story of years of false starts and "back to the drawing board". She spent hours giving me all the bad news, "the return on this project is too low, your team is poor, the engineers are lazy, supply management is embarrassingly bad..." on and on she went.

While many people would have gotten dismayed, I saw this as an opportunity to prove myself. I wanted to be the guy that finally led this to market...no...I was GOING to be the guy that finally took this to market. In addition, I resolved to never talk about the team this way. Each person had something valuable to bring to the group, and I wanted to find that and bring it out of them, not put them down at every opportunity.

After a few weeks, I finally started taking over the meetings and working on the plan. For weeks I kept a positive attitude and kept pushing the team. You could have cut the skepticism with a knife. I'm not sure that anyone in the group believed that this project would ever actually come to fruition. Trying to motivate people to do quality work, when they feel like they're wasting their time is a special kind of leadership challenge.

I knew I had to keep the final goal in mind and keep a positive attitude. All naysayers I met with complete confidence and assurance that this project would move forward. Each hurdle, I confronted with poise and conviction that we would find a resolution.

Meanwhile, in the background, I kept open communication with senior leaders, gauging their receptivity at every step. The same confidence and positivity about the project that I exhumed with my team, I carried into my conversations with leaders as well. All the while, I was using these conversations to better understand the reasons behind the "no" that this project kept getting, then using that information to relay to my team how we needed to present our proposal.

Finally, the day came to present the project. I knew which direction our leadership was going to lean, but because of their personalities, I also knew that they needed to see options. That day, over the next 8 hours, weeks of work culminated with four different courses of action for our leadership to pick.

The team had been through this ringer several times before. It was a critical moment, several key members in the team had gotten on board and we were starting to click as a group. As we approached the end of the presentation, and we arrived at the decision slide, I stood up in front of the directors:

"Gentlemen, I implore you to make a decision today. This team has been through this presentation several times. They have explored every possible option. They have looked at every angle. What you have in front of you are the only four ways of doing this program. Each has a set of pros and cons which we have presented to you today. I can't stress enough how important it is that we leave today with a decision. We have snacks in the back, I am prepared to purchase dinner, answer questions, or be here as long as it takes, but we have to make a decision today. This team cannot go back to the drawing board again. That is not an option. You must pick from one of the four courses of action in front of you."

I sat down, this was it, and I put it all out on the table. I showed my team that I was willing to go down with them. I stood in front of people that far outranked me and gave them an ultimatum. One which I had absolutely no authority to give, but I delivered it with the same poise and certainty that I had used to lead this team to this point.

Eventually the directors asked to have everyone leave so they could discuss further, then around dinner time, I was summoned to the room. They had arrived at a decision, but before I told the team, they needed to inform the Vice President who was out of the country. The final decision would not come until the next day, but I'm still counting it as a victory.

They picked the smallest scope that cost the least amount of money to create. Our plan was to bring the product to market in 18 months. The project that sat on the shelf for years was called "Thunder". We renamed the project "Lightning", a very real action, with powerful results, high electric energy, and in a short time.

Over the next year and a half, that team delivered tremendous results. The morale was a peak, and other employees in the building *wanted* to be on our team. Those same people, the "low performers" stepped up in tremendous ways. We were clicking well together, and soon project lightning would go to market. It surpassed every expectation and metric that was defined at the key meeting when the project was approved. It stayed on schedule, under budget, and delivered return on investment almost three times what was expected!

There were a lot of things that went our way over the course of two years, some of it was luck, much of it was leadership, but none of it would have happened without a confident can-do attitude to act as the spark to start the flame.

There will always be problems, things will go wrong, sometimes, even with the best effort and the winningest attitude, you will still fail. I can guarantee, however, that if you *don't* have a great attitude, your chances of failure go up exponentially. Your crappy defeatist attitude isn't inspiring anyone.

Take Action:
Are you using negative words to describe your team? The truth is that teams are a reflection of their leader, so what does that say about you? For the next month, make an effort to change your phrases. Rather than call someone lazy, take ownership and say, "I need to find a way to motivate them more." Instead of saying someone is stupid say, "Let's find out what they are really good at." Try it for an entire month!

3. Initiative

Iraq, 2007

We were a few months into my Iraq deployment when I was placed as the assistant planning officer. It was one of those positions where you have a lot of responsibility but essentially no authority. Generally, it's a role for Captains to fill before they take command of a company.

I was resolved to be the greatest planner possible. My competitive spirit drove me to push harder and faster than all those before me. Rather than rely on any natural talent that I was not gifted, I was certain that hard work would get me ahead.

As soon as tasks were given to me, I would delve deeply into them, and made absolutely certain that they were done in record time with impeccable quality. Then I would quickly inform my boss that the work was complete and ask for my next task. Like this, the cycle continued.

"I'm done, what's next?"

Get task, finish.

"I'm done, what's next?"

Get task, finish.

"I'm done, what's next?"

So it continued, until finally one day, my boss Major Schreiner looked at me over his computer. His eyes locked with mine, his hands never left his keyboard, and he dropped a bomb on me that changed my life in an instant:

"You have access to the calendar Louis. Look at it and figure out what's next."

His eyes dropped back down to the computer, and I remember the clacking of his laptop as I spun slowly in my chair to stare back at my own screen. I'm sure if I asked him, he wouldn't even remember the interaction, but to me, it was life changing. He was absolutely right!

Here I was, in my own mind, telling myself what an awesome job I was doing. Meanwhile, I wasn't much more than a second pair of hands. I wasn't contributing to the mission at all. They weren't getting my best brain power, in fact, they were getting very little of it.

I had taken zero initiative for weeks. None!

How could I possibly be successful as a leader if I was incapable of making even the smallest decision like "what's next?" I realized at that moment, that if I was actually going to lead, if I was actually going to make a difference, I had to lead myself.

At that very moment, I began a journey of change. It was as if I had been a dog on a leash my whole life, and now, this Major just took the leash off. It was time for me to run on my own. I understood the mission well, in fact, I had penned the entire order. I was intimately familiar with the commander's intent. I knew what I had the authority to do. I knew what needed to be done, and I knew what the end state was. So off I went.

That was the last time I ever asked Major Schreiner "what's next?" From then on, I operated freely, wholly on initiative, executing tasks towards the mission and goal of the unit. It was scary at first, sometimes I missed the mark, but overall, I did my best work when I was free.

In the years since, the principle of "you have access to the calendar" has often been in the back of my mind. I arrive at a new position, and I start by defining the goals of the company, factory, store, etc. I make sure that I understand the intent of my boss and his boss, all the way to the top. I make sure to understand where my authority ends, then I get to work.

I want you to understand something: There is always something to do.

If ever you are at work, or at home, and you are feeling "bored", then you are not taking initiative; you are not leading yourself. If you have finished your own work, help someone around you. If you are home, get a book and learn something.

Social Media is fun. I genuinely enjoy it. In it I find plenty of things that make me laugh, connect me with people whom I love, and keep me involved in current events. I even run a rather large page for my other book CONUS Battle Drills which brings me great joy in helping veterans in their transition to civilian life. That being said, most of our engagement on these platforms is a waste of time.

I want you to think about the tasks you perform every day, especially on your off time: watch movies, TV, sports, Facebook, Twitter, drink, whatever. Now ask yourself this question: "If I stopped doing this, would my life change at all?"

I used to be a big football fan. I loved the Miami Dolphins, and I loved watching Dan Marino play. I always wanted him to earn a Super Bowl ring and go down in history as one of the greatest players in the game. I knew every player, every statistic, I would spend hours watching games on the weekends.

It was Marino's last game, a playoff game against the Jacksonville Jaguars. I was in the living room of my aunt's house in Miami, and we were all very excited and hopeful, coming off a playoff win, that this would actually be the year Marino would get his ring.

It wasn't.

In fact, Miami was defeated in one of the worst losses of any team in the history of the NFL playoffs. It was embarrassing, and a sad way for a great player to end his career. I watched every second of the game, always believing that there was a chance.

That night I lay in my bed, distraught, with actual butterflies in my stomach, physically reacting to this loss. Then I had an epiphany: Dan Marino didn't give a crap about me. He was still a millionaire, and my life would be exactly the same tomorrow as it was today, despite what a bunch of grown men did playing a football game. That very night, I realized how much of my time and energy this useless activity was sucking up.

It was the last NFL game that I ever watched from start to finish, and honestly, my life is still completely unaffected by what happens on that field every Sunday.

So ask yourself again: "If I stopped doing this, would my life change at all?"

For instance, if you stop doing the dishes, your life is going to change. If you stop showering, your life is going to change. If you stop eating healthy or exercising, your life is going to change. If you stop watching sports, or spending hours on Instagram, is your life going to change?

For me, I realized that football was a waste of my time and started leading myself to more productive endeavors with my newfound hours. Today I need to constantly fight the urge to peruse Facebook in search of nothing, finding nothing, and losing precious time where I could be improving myself.

When I know that I should be looking at the calendar to find out "what's next", I find myself reaching for the phone to kill time (which is really quite stupid). It is in that moment of temptation that I have to make the decision if I want to truly be a leader. If you're here, then you're over 6,000 words into this book, so it's probably safe to assume that you want to be a leader no? So are you leading yourself? Are you taking the initiative to look at the calendar to find what's next? Or are you allowing yourself to be consumed by wasteful behaviors accomplishing nothing and moving yourself nowhere with your precious time?

Stop waiting to be told what to do. Even if you do those things better than anyone else, it's really not impressive. Take the initiative, find what's next on the calendar, stop wasting your time, and start leading yourself.

Take Action:

Find one thing you are doing right now that isn't making you better. Get wild with it, delete the Facebook or Twitter app from your phone, and schedule the time of day when you're going to get on there. If it's not hours of social media, maybe it's something else. Regardless, find that thing, then replace it with something that is going to make you better.

4. Honor, Integrity, and Commitment

Arizona, 2009

"We need to talk"

I had just come out of the gym with my buddy when I got the voicemail from a cute girl who I'd been in a very casual relationship with. My heart sank, I wasn't sure what the news was going to be, but based on the decisions we had been making to that point, it probably wasn't "good" (at least as I defined it at that time in my life). We agreed to meet up and she came into my apartment. I sat on the couch opposite her, "I'm pregnant, I don't need you around, but I'm having this baby." I'm sure there were many more words said, but I was in such a state of fear and shock, those were really the only ones that remained in my memory. She grabbed her stuff, wiped her eyes, and walked out. I don't remember if I said anything at all.

At that point, I already had military orders for my next duty station, and was only days away from moving cross country from Arizona to Maryland. The trip was over 2,300 miles and I spent most of the drive in silence; my brain was working in overtime.

I called my grandmother to tell her the news. I told her with absolute certainty that I simply wasn't going to marry someone just because she was pregnant. I could hear her smile through the phone as she told me in Spanish, "Ok, well, you pray for your thing, and I'll pray for my thing." I didn't really do much praying in those days, I was more of a Christian in name only. My grandmother on the other hand, seems to have a red phone to the big man himself based on the frequency with which her prayers come to fruition.

But I am a very stubborn man.

At first I called back to Tucson once a month, then every couple weeks, then every week, and within a few months, I would get off work and rush to make a phone call on my way home. I was so excited to talk to this girl who was quite an incredible woman. She had courage and poise. She was tough and honest. She was beautiful and loving. Most of all, she could handle me, the arrogant twice deployed Airborne Ranger who was a hero in his own mind.

At some point in those months of talking, I realized: This little boy had not asked to come into this world. I had the choice of being selfish, continuing with my destructive lifestyle, or leading myself, and becoming the father that this new life deserved.

I made my decision, I committed, and I proposed to this amazing woman; that was nine years ago as of this writing.

In that time I have learned a lot about relationships. I watched and learned from those who had made it decades and realized that they were truly committed to their marriages. Rather than looking at the relationship like a contract (make me happy and I'll stay married to you), they approached it like a covenant (I will do what it takes to make this work).

These people stand out in our world of self-serving, instant gratification, and extremely little self-leadership. In a world where a single post results in an "unfollow" or "unfriend", people are approaching their relationships with the same carelessness. How often do you hear "s/he doesn't make me happy anymore." This is the self-serving manner in which millions approach their marriages. Their faithfulness is predicated on a need to be satisfied by their partner, never willing to ask the question, "am I doing everything I can to make my partner happy?"

If you want to really stand out and learn leadership, start being a leader in your relationships. Show honor and integrity every moment of your life. This isn't something you can turn on and off, you must *live* it.

Sometimes, in leadership, you will have to "win over" employees who have lost their morale and are only biding time (either to retirement or to move on). These people will give you very few reasons to stay motivated. Often they do not thank you for your efforts, they will find the negative in most situations, they are slow to action, and generally bring everyone else down. As a leader, you have a responsibility to your team. That responsibility exists whether or not the team "makes you happy". Before you can look to anyone else to change, you have to change. You have to decide and commit to excellence. You have to respond with kindness, surety, confidence, poise, firmness, fairness, and integrity, no matter how you are approached.

My mother used to tell me growing up, "Keep your words soft and sweet because you never know when you are going to have to eat them." It turns out the advice was sage. Every time I have lost my cool, responded in anger, stooped down to meet the level at which I was approached, I have lost the high ground. No matter who was right, I was wrong.

When I committed to being a husband, father, and leader at home, my leadership at work grew exponentially as well. Every waking moment of my life, I was being trained on the principles of leadership. It went from being a persona or a character that I played at work, to a part of my actual self. The gravity of that realization, of the importance of the skill, drove me to get better.

When I was just a young boy, maybe ten or eleven years old, I lied to my father about something. I can't remember what the lie was, and it didn't really matter, what mattered was that I had lied. I remember standing halfway up our marble staircase in Rota, Spain holding the wrought iron handrail looking down at my father on the landing. He looked at me with piercing hazel eyes that stared right into my soul and gave me a chance, "Are you sure that's what happened?" He gave me an opportunity to tell the truth, but I didn't take it, instead I set myself on a path to learn a valuable life lesson. "Yes, that's what happened," I answered less confident this time. He shook his head in palpable disappointment, "go to your room, I need to think."

I sat in my room on the edge of my bed quietly and anxiously awaiting my sentence. It seemed like hours before he came in (although it was probably only a few minutes) and he sat down in the bed next to me. "Son, do you know what your most prized possession is," he asked somberly. I looked around my room, staring at my toys, my radio, whatever nick-knack was around looking for an answer. "It's not in your room son, it's your principles. You see, men can take all this from you," he motioned around the room. "They can take your stuff, they can take your family, they can even take your life, but *your principles*, are only yours to give away. No man can take your principles from you, and that is why you should cherish them, hold them dear, and never EVER give them up." At that moment, as a young boy, all the stories of sacrifice and tribulation my family faced escaping Cuba finally came to a head. This lesson, which was being imparted on me through a simple grounding for a couple months, was learned by my father through great pain. To this day, stories of men boldly facing execution only resolve to reaffirm this lesson: your principles are only yours to give away.

Being a man or woman of honor and integrity is so much more than just telling the truth regardless if anyone is watching. How much time do you spend actually doing your job? Not being at work, but actually working. This would exclude your lunches, your breaks, the time you spend on the internet, the non-work-related conversations, etc. At home, how much time are you devoted to your family? Are you continuing those poor habits and stopping at the bar every day before you get home? Do you spend time on your phone instead of engaging your family? Are you more interested in the latest sports event than spending time with your children?

Some of you are really judging other readers right now because you feel you are very involved with your family, "This doesn't apply to me at all," you've told yourself. I ask you, how much fruitful work are you doing? Have you improved the efficiency of your work or delegated tasks to take on more, or do you fill the hours at the office with busy work? Are you really creating value for your employer? How many value-add, productive, tasks are you doing? When you're at home, are you taking the time to build relationships, or are you busy with "tasks" that have to get done? Shuttling kids from one activity to the next? Do your conversations only focus on the next event or task that you have to go to?

In both cases, you are a thief. You are stealing from your employer and your family. You are either unplugged or spinning out of control. Truly great leaders make themselves available, but they stay busy. You must have the integrity not to steal, the honor to make time for what is truly important, and the commitment to follow through when it gets hard. You must stop pretending to be a leader and embrace the role in everything you do. Take the opportunity to learn from your family, no one else will be ask forgiving as your child.

The rewards for your actions will be immeasurable. My three children are the greatest gift I could ever have received. If I had known the day I got the "we have to talk" call about the great joy my family would bring, I would have been elated at the news instead of scared! My wife tells our oldest boy that his "superpower" is that he made us a family.

Being a great leader is going to require a lot of work and self-leadership. Internalizing these lessons and applying them to everything you do is going to be hard. That being said, your rewards will be even bigger. Financially you are going to be rewarded with greater responsibility, and at home, you are going to be rewarded with meaningful, fruitful, fulfilling relationships that give you more drive and purpose to push further!

Take Action:

Schedule out your day. Not just the meetings you need to attend, but the other work you need to do also. Put time on your calendar for all those menial tasks you keep putting off.

5. Get your money right

Iowa, 2011

I was leading an assembly line in a manufacturing facility as my first job coming out of the military. In many ways, it felt like being a platoon leader again. The pay was decent, but the real financial reward was coming from all the overtime hours I was working. Fifty hours a week was the minimum, most weeks I was pushing 80-90 hours, which meant my overtime checks were significant. This, combined with years of poor money education, resulted in a fair bit of complacency in my expenses.

After a couple of years of long hours, while being a full time MBA student, and having a child in the middle, I was mentally and physically beat. I was desperate for a change, and a different kind of challenge. I took a lateral position in a Marketing role. My days were much shorter, the overtime was gone, but so was the pay.

This would start one of the most trying seasons of my marriage. Overnight, we lost thousands of dollars a month in pay. In addition, I was traveling for weeks at a time, all while my wife was taking care of a newborn at home. We watched in horror as our accounts continued to get lower and lower, and neither of us knew what was going on.

There is a fundamental deficiency in money education in our world today. I recently saw an article on USA today that detailed a chart of debt that the average US Household has, and the numbers were appalling:

- $17,000 in Credit Cards
- $30,000 in Auto Loans
- $50,000 in student loans
- $180,000 Mortgage

All of this on a $60,000 a year income!! For some reason, we have allowed our consumption to drive us into massive amounts of debt, slaves to our debtors and completely lost control of our money.

My wife and I were in a similar situation, but we didn't have large credit card debt or student loans. We realized that one of the major sources of strife in our marriage at this time was the fact that we were not able to save any money, and we were losing money every month. Like most Americans, we didn't have a budget, and rather than telling our money where to go, we were just looking at the bottom number every month. It was time for a drastic change!

We sat down on the dining room table and looked at our accounts for the previous couple months. What we found was very disturbing: we were spending more money every month than we were bringing in. It was time to buckle down and buckle down hard.

We got rid of cable and went to internet only. I stopped buying lunch and started taking leftovers from the night before. We made a strict entertainment budget that allowed us one day a week to go out for dinner (sometimes two). I got rid of my truck and closed a no growth retirement account to pay off the second car. By doing that, we eliminated two car payments. That alone saved us nearly $1,000 a month. We started building money saving habits and had a detailed budget.

For the first time, we were telling our money where to go, instead of finding out where it went.

We made our habits part of our lifestyle, and through years of work, we now have over six months of pay saved up, plus we are able to be more charitable than ever before! It is true freedom and exciting!

You might be asking, "What does all of this have to do with leadership?"

Well, let me first give you a counter-example. Imagine you are a hiring manager and you have the option of hiring two people to manage a department. One of these people has significant money problems. He lives hand-to-mouth, is always complaining about not having enough money, and yet you see some continuing bad money habits: eats out every day, has multiple cars and car payments, the latest phone, gadgets, grown up toys like boats, motorcycles, etc. Overall, he practices terrible money management skills in his personal life. Just on that description alone, are you more or less inclined to give that person Profit & Loss (P&L) responsibility in your business? Generally, the answer is no. If he can't manage his personal finances with great care and responsibility, chances are, he's going to be just as reckless with the budget of your business.

There's more than just the perception that he is going to be reckless with your business, there is also the second and third order effects it has on professionalism and conduct in the workplace.

Someone who is not financially responsible is also fearful and they bring that with them into the office. Rumors of any sort that involve cutting hours, or pay, will flourish because he will always lend them credence out of his own fear. This person is also more likely to abuse overtime because more income is seen as the only way to survive.

I also want you to consider the impact this type of person in a leadership role has to their employees. If your manager was always complaining about how they didn't have enough money, how would that make you feel? Is that motivating in any way whatsoever? Of course not. Your manager presumably makes more than you, and if you can make your income work, but your manager can't, he will instantly lose credibility in your eyes. It's immature and irresponsible, and any conversation or correction they attempt to administer that relates to financial matters in the workplace will be dripping with so much irony that you will respond with apathy at best and disgust at worst.

This is probably tough for many of you to hear, especially considering that most people reading this will be in some form of debt and lack the savings to deal with financial catastrophes. This book, however, isn't intended to make you feel great about your skills. The intent of this book is to teach you how to be a truly great leader!

While most of the advice given here can be implemented rather quickly, in matters of finances, turning around years of debt accumulation doesn't happen overnight. What can happen overnight is how you communicate your financial standing in the workplace. First, stop talking about your financial state (particularly if it's less than stellar). Second, don't allow fear to rule you when you hear rumors of pay, squash them quickly with confidence. Third, if you have taken a second job to supplement your income due to your debt, keep it to yourself. Fourth, if you have made stupid financial decisions or inane expenditures, there's no need to share that with anyone else. Fifth and finally, get yourself on the path to financial freedom. There are plenty of resources available to help you learn how to budget and start telling your money where to go instead of finding out where it went.

If you want to be recognized as an outstanding leader, you are going to have to get your money right!

Take Action:

Pull up your account statements for the past three months. Look at where your money is going and make a list of all your expenses. Now decide what you can cut out, then repurpose that money towards paying off debt or savings. In a few years you will be able to experience financial freedom.

6. Set Your Goals

Fort Benning, 2004

"Gentlemen, in front of you is a packet of papers. The top page is a Ranger release form. It is a form stating that you volunteer to go to Ranger School. Ranger school is not a requirement for infantry officers. Every one of you will go. Sign the form and pass it to the center…Now, Welcome to the Infantry Officer Basic Course!"

It was June 6th, 2004. I remember that particular date distinctly because it was the 60th anniversary of D-Day, a Sunday, and my very first day as an officer in the United States Army. It was my own personal D-Day, and it happened to fall on the Lord's special day as well. Those words above were the very first words spoken to me. I remember sitting next to my best friend Chad Shields and the two of us chuckling at the irony of being required to volunteer for one of the toughest schools in the entire US Army. It didn't matter to us though, we had volunteered for the infantry, and both of us had elected the 82nd Airborne division as our first choice of unit because we both wanted to be as close to combat as possible.

We went through the basic course without a hitch, and then me, Chad, and a handful of other officers that were slated to go to units that were deploying, graduated a few days early so we could report to the Ranger Training Battalion and start the grueling course.

The night before, we checked and re-checked our bags, shaved our heads (it was a requirement), and laid in bed staring at the ceiling feigning sleep. The next morning we arrived at Camp Rogers along with over 350 other Ranger hopefuls and fell into formation long before the sun rose.

The first week of Ranger school at the time was the Ranger Assessment and Preparation or RAP week phase. It consisted of a series of pass or fail events designed to weed out the weakest first. We didn't even unpack our bags before we took our physical fitness test.

While we were familiar with the format, the grading of the events at Ranger school were notoriously stringent. A push-up and sit-up had to be absolutely perfect in order to be counted. Many soldiers throughout the Army, who had taken that test any number of times at their units, were unable to make the minimum requirements. As the early morning test progressed, more and more soldiers were filling the "retest" lines because they didn't pass.

In addition, Ranger school added one more event: the pull-up which happened immediately following the two mile run event. In order to pass, the Ranger had to complete 6 perfect pull-ups all the way up, hold, and all the way down, pause. It was my weakest event, and it was the first time I almost got kicked out of Ranger school. On my sixth pull-up, I instinctively kicked my legs and the instructor did not count it. By this point I was completely smoked, it was only through sheer willpower and determination that I managed to pull off one more and joined the ranks of ear to ear smiles of those who passed. By the time the sun was up, dozens of Rangers were already disqualified from the course, and we numbered fewer than 300.

The rest of the week would not get any easier. I busted my knee on the land navigation course and finished with less than ten seconds to spare (I heard the countdown over the radio as I turned in my scorecard). We ran 5 miles through hurricane Jeanne (maybe a tropical depression by that point). I had to re-try several obstacles on the obstacle course because I could not cross them easily, and I pulled a muscle in my back during the 15 mile road march so badly that I could barely see through the pain coursing in my body…. but I had a goal in mind and I was GOING to get my Ranger tab.

When I had completed RAP week, it was a huge sigh of relief. There were less than 200 of us by the end of that first week (I'm not sure of the exact count); it looked as though we had lost nearly half the class.

It was at this point that the instructors, who had a special talent for creating chaos and stress, congratulated those of us that remained. They told us that now…*now*…Ranger school began. For the next two months we would go through a series of progressively more difficult patrols while alternating leadership positions, sometimes even mid-mission. Because of this, we all had to pay close attention to what was going on because we never knew when we would be selected to lead the mission. Our meals came once or twice a day, and sleep would come even more rarely. We would spend time in Fort Benning, a few weeks in the Appalachian Mountains, and a few weeks in swamps in Florida. All the while, at every single moment, for over 60 days, we were always being evaluated. Any misstep could receive a negative spot report, and too many of those would get you kicked out of the course.

I had a special propensity and skill for acquiring these negative spot reports due to my "outgoing" nature and inability to shut my damn mouth. As a result, I was given a "favor" by the instructors in the mountains and afforded the opportunity of re-taking the second phase and extending my stay in Ranger school by several weeks. This is to say I failed the mountain phase and had to retake it.

My second time through the mountain phase was exponentially more difficult than the first. Besides the mental beat down I took from knowing that everything I had endured the first time through was for naught, the weather in November in the mountains was particularly unforgiving. We endured days of non-stop rain with temperatures in the 30's and then finally, on Thanksgiving Day 2004, the rain relented, and it snowed. I will never forget the extremely bitter and painful cold of standing completely naked in the snow putting on sopping wet polypropylene and gortex uniforms to trudge all day through the snow.

The swamps in Florida weren't much more forgiving. When we arrived, we were given special instruction on what to do in the event that we were separated from the group. Several years earlier four students died of hypothermia in chest deep swamp water and by the time we went, special care and rules were developed to ensure it didn't happen again. One of those rules concerned the temperature of the water, unfortunately for us, the water stayed *just* above the minimum requirement and we froze our butts off through hours of mucky, muddy, gator infested, Florida swamp water.

One mission took us particularly close to the civilian population. I could see, from my position, the Christmas lights of decorated houses just a couple hundred yards away. I remember imagining what those families might be doing at that moment, warm, fed, loved, and was quickly snapped back into reality as I had to slosh through waist deep freezing water to pull our zodiac boat out of a sandbar. It would have been so easy to quit at that moment. I could have stopped the pain, ended the hunger, gotten some sleep, but I had a goal. I had resolved that I would leave Ranger school dead before I left without my tab, and so, in December of 2004, myself and 72 other soldiers out of the original 350+ earned the coveted Ranger tab and learned several valuable life lessons that I impart to you today.

I'm sure you've heard about SMART goals. These are goals that are Specific, Measurable, Achievable, Realistic, and Time based. SMART goals are crap. It's a methodology that encourages and rewards mediocrity. You want to feel good about staying in the same place and not making major waves? Set SMART goals. If instead, you want to make a difference, grow a company, change your life or someone else's, then stay away from SMART goals, instead set crazy goals; here's how…

First, set goals that scare you. The most valuable achievements I have earned in life have come from setting goals that kept me awake at night. Getting married, being a father to my children, changing my career, financial peace, all of these goals were set long before I had a plan to achieve them and they were scary. People that achieve greatness don't do it by setting easy goals that don't challenge them, they do it by setting goals that few other people will even attempt. In America in particular, it's the bold that are rewarded. People like

Oprah, Bezos, Gates, Jobs, Musk, and more set outrageous, scary, goals!

Second, resolve and commit to achieving your goals at all costs. The path to greatness is never easy, in fact, it usually gets much harder right before you emerge victorious. Talk to a couple that has been married for 40 or 50 years, often you will find there was a time of great tribulation in their relationship, often at the cusp of divorce, through which they slogged right before they found their "secret" to a long and rewarding relationship. Talk to multi-millionaires and you will often hear a story about rock-bottom at the precipice of failure right before their greatest success. Everyone who has achieved a scary goal has suffered numerous setbacks along the way, setbacks that would deter most from continuing, but through their own determination and grit, they pushed through and made it.

Third and finally, you are capable of so much more than you think. I went into Ranger school thinking I knew what my physical and mental limits were. Then the instructors pushed me past that point. Then they took me further still. Then finally, they pushed me so far that I could no longer remember what my limitations were and I realized that there wasn't actually a limit; the only limitation was in my own mind.

I want you to truly believe in yourself. I want you to shut out those pesky voices that tell you you're not good enough, you're not smart enough, you're not educated enough, or whatever other crap rattles around in your noggin when things get hard. Murder the excuses and thoughts of mediocrity that attempt to take root. Set that goal that is so scary it forces sleep to elude you. Resolve to achieve that goal, no matter what, and remember that you are capable of so much more than you know.

Your limitations are imaginary!

Take Action:

Sit down and set one crazy scary goal. Don't put a time limit on it, but write down what actions you need to take in order to accomplish your crazy scary goal. Now make sure you stay on it!

7. Be the Best

Spain, 1993

Like most teenagers, I had a tendency to cut corners with chores and keep my room in disrepair. I don't remember the particular event, or what it was that drove my mother to employ a different tactic with me, but I have to thank her for the patience she exhibited. She likely made up the following story, but it changed my behavior in countless areas of my life.

"I want to tell you a story about a poor woman," she began. "This woman didn't really have an education, and not very many skills. The only thing she really knew how to do was to cook and clean, and so she got a job in a hotel as a maid. She made it her mission to learn her trade better than anyone else. Every time she entered a room, she made sure every detail was perfect. The beds had perfect corners and were so tight you could bounce a quarter off of them. The rooms were completely vacuumed so not a single speck of dust remained. She cleaned every surface. She put the soaps in exactly the right spots and with great care. She folded the towels into beautiful shapes, and she even folded the toilet paper into a little triangle. Every room, every day, every time, was always perfect. As time went on, she got better and faster.

"One day this hotel chain had a competition. They wanted to see who could turn a room the fastest with the greatest amount of accuracy to their expectations. This lady entered the competition and blew everyone away. She was twice as fast as anyone else, and when it was done, her rooms were perfect! That maid won the competition and got a big promotion training all the other maids in the hotel chain. She ended up making more money than anyone had ever made in her family and grew to a high leadership position in that company. All of it because she decided to take the extra care in doing things perfectly!

"Here's what I want you to remember son: I don't care if you make beds for a living, you make the best beds anyone ever has!"

Regardless of whether the story was true or not, the lesson was exceptionally valuable: No matter what you do, do it better than anyone else. From that moment on, my work ethic changed from dispassionate teenager to zealous perfectionist, and it has served me well throughout my career. Granted, some days I was better than others (it happens to all of us), but if it was my job, I was going to do it better than anyone else.

If anything requires you to lead yourself, it's going to be the way you treat the little things. While most maids just made the bed to the minimum standard, the maid from our parable had perfect hospital corners and a bed so tight you could bounce a quarter off it. Let me ask you something, if your job starts at 8am, are you arriving somewhere between 8:00 and 8:05? Or are you there ten minutes early ready to start work at 8am? If your job requires you to make a

PowerPoint presentation, do you make sure that you have the exact same font and formatting in every slide? Do you rehearse your presentation? Do you print out copies of relevant information as handouts? Are you in the room before everyone else getting it set up and making sure everything works? Are you thinking through every detail shooting for perfection every time?

Great leaders go the extra mile always. Their work is untouchable. They are punctual, they are always dressed appropriately. They show up early and stay late. They make time for everyone. They don't miss deadlines. They are not sloppy with their person or their product. They are efficient and always seem to get more done than everyone else. They don't engage in office gossip. They live professionalism in everything they do...always.

Great leaders understand that everyone is watching all the time. Being a great leader is not a nine-to-five position, it's a 24/7 position. Granted, even great leaders make mistakes and have their personality flaws, but it's only by shooting for perfection at all times, leading yourself at all times, that you will even come close to becoming the person that everyone wants to follow.

You need to make yourself irreplaceable, and it starts by making the best metaphorical bed that anyone has ever made.

I want you to take some time for honest self-reflection. I want you to think about how you conduct yourself on a daily basis and consider whether you are really giving it everything you have. Are you honestly putting forth the best effort, with cautious attention to detail, in every aspect of your life?

Let me put this another way, would you want to work for yourself? Are you the husband or wife that you would want or that you would want for your children? Are you being the best parent you can be or are you prioritizing other unimportant things over your family? Are you the employee you would want working for you?

If you would not accept your behaviors from the people around you, then it's time you start leading yourself. It's time you start setting those goals and achieving them. It's time you act like a professional, like an expert, like the best maid. If you want to be a great leader, then you need to become one. Stop looking at external forces, stop making excuses for yourself. Everyone has tough times and tribulations.

Great leaders don't accept that they are just making beds, they are disgusted by mediocrity, and you should be too.

Take Action:

What are you cutting corners on? Usually it's something we don't want to do, or don't like doing. This week, identify one thing you're doing that you know you can do better. Now resolve to focus on that task, execute it when you have high energy (like the morning at the start of the week), and put everything into it.

8. Conquer your fear

Afghanistan, 2005

"The base is under attack!"

Sergeant Harvey Lewis stormed into our sleeping area, banging the metal door to our concrete room against the wall as he ran back to his cot to get his gear. We slept with almost 30 men in a single room built with solid walls designed to keep bullets and shrapnel from penetrating into our sleeping area. Usually an "attack" meant mortar or rocket fire which came with the familiar sounds of whooshes and booms which I didn't hear. In my sleep stupor, my first thought was "what is he talking about?" because I didn't hear the explosions I expected.

My cot was closest to the door, so I stood up and pushed the door open, and in an instant the gravity of the situation settled deep into my gut. What I saw were hundreds of tracer rounds pinging against the rocks right outside the door. It took less than a second, I turned and flipped on the lights and boomed in a loud voice, "direct fire, let's go!" I spun around quickly, slipped my feet into my boots, threw on a jacket, tossed my body armor on, snapped in my night vision, grabbed my rifle, and charged out the door without looking behind me; less than a minute had gone by.

It was December 22nd, 2005. Our outpost was within a couple kilometers from the Pakistan border at about 6,000 feet elevation. The air was cold, and a few inches of snow covered the ground. I was still wearing shorts, no socks, and a thin jacket over a t-shirt. My boots weren't tied, I only pulled the shoe strings tight and shoved the length into the boots themselves. As I exited the door I tried to assess where the tracer rounds were coming from; at this point I didn't know if there were enemy inside the base or not, which meant every movement was a potential target.

I could hear the familiar sound of an AK-47 firing very close nearby, which only served to confirm that the enemy had made it into the base. The volume of rounds was significant, and with each step I realized the enemy force had to be in the hundreds. I continued stepping forward, my thumb was pressed securely on the selector switch of my weapon, ready to click from "safe" to "semi" in a fraction of a second. We had trained so much that switching off "safe" and pulling the trigger was an action I could complete virtually simultaneously.

I moved alongside the building, using it for cover from plunging fire, rounds pinging off the rocks just inches away as I moved towards the AK fire. The moon was bright, and I had a monocular night vision device that I wore over my left eye, which allowed me to keep peripheral vision on my right side and look directly at the ground below me. I caught some movement and spun quickly, raising my weapon while squeezing the pressure switch on the front handle of my weapon that turned on an infrared laser which stopped center mass on the target. My target did the exact same motion and each of us was staring at a laser center mass on our respective bodies. Instantly we both knew we were on the same side, lasers turned off, and we turned to move towards the enemy.

I reached the end of the building, there was about a 10-foot gap in-between buildings and I could tell the AK sound was just around the corner. I was careful not to allow the barrel of my weapon flag around the corner and held the rifle tightly against my body. Less than two minutes had passed since SGT Lewis stormed into hooch, and I was about to come face first with the enemy. Even through the sound of gunfire, I could hear my platoon pouring out of the building behind me, and the fear set in quickly. I stopped for a moment, took a breath, let it out hard, and spun around the corner. My thumb clicked the safety off as I brought my weapon up to the target and squeezed my laser on. My finger dropped down onto the trigger lightly and I found my target. The laser stopped center mass, and right before I pulled the trigger I stopped.

The small base we were on had less than 100 US soldiers on it, guys from the 82nd Airborne, 173rd Airborne Field Artillery, and US Special Forces. It was a badass group of guys who were zealous fighters. Because of the small number, we also used Afghan forces to man our walls and provide security while we took the fight to the enemy. I was staring at one such Afghan soldier, with his eyes closed, and his rifle over the wall firing blindly in the general direction of the attack. He was not in his assigned post and had no idea how close he came to getting shot.

I finally had a moment to analyze the battle and see the scope of what we were up against. Hundreds of enemy fighters had crossed the Afghanistan/Pakistan border in a coordinated attack in the middle of the night. They had managed to overrun an observation post and were making their way down the high ground towards our base, getting to within 100 meters of our outer wall. They outnumbered us 3 or 4 to one and had plunging fire on our position. What they didn't count on was the ferocity of the 100 men on that small base.

In just a few minutes we had amassed our forces and subordinate leaders started working together, running in between positions through a hail of gunfire, getting on the correct radio frequencies, updating on our respective positions, and establishing a battle plan on the fly. We fought for hours, eventually repelling the enemy attack. Not a single US Soldier was killed that night, the enemy was not as lucky. It was an amazing display of courage and leadership by every single one of them, and to this day, I am so incredibly proud to have been there to witness it.

Being in the Army taught me a lot about managing fear. Anyone that ever tells you they weren't afraid is lying. I am deathly afraid of heights. One of the hardest days in Ranger school for me was the water confidence day. You have to climb up to a log 35 feet above the water and walk across it, stepping up two steps in the middle, then shimmy on a rope, then drop into the water. The step isn't particularly secure, and there is nothing to hold onto. You then climb a 70-foot latter, grab a pulley, and slide down a cable to the water below. For someone like me, who is nearly paralyzed by my fear of heights, stepping forward in the face of that fear was a nearly insurmountable challenge. I faced that same fear later in Airborne operations, jumping out of a plane at 800-1,000 feet. That familiar sense of dread, deep in the pit of my stomach, hit me as I stood at the edge of that building in Afghanistan. By this point in my life, however, I had trained myself to allow that fear to exist, but move forward in spite of it.

Some of my life's greatest accomplishments have been when I embraced that fear and stepped forward. I earned my Ranger tab, Airborne wings, and brought all my guys home from multiple combat deployments because I did not allow fear to control me. Since then, I have encountered fear in the workplace, never as intense, but that familiar tingle has served as a motivator instead of a paralyzer. Speaking in public, disciplining an employee, confronting a boss, starting a new job, all of these events create fear in us. If you want to be a leader, you need to step forward in the face of that fear.

You need to lead your team, and sometimes that means getting rid of a bad employee who simply can't be mentored. Sometimes it means confronting a decision your manager has made. Sometimes it means supporting a potentially unpopular decision. Often it means recognizing your fear, but not allowing yourself to be paralyzed by it. No one has accomplished anything great by succumbing to fear, but *everyone* who as accomplished something great has felt that fear.

Do not listen to the lies your scared brain is telling you. Instead, when you feel that fear setting in, know that it's time to act.

Arizona 2017

We were in a shift changeover meeting when I was in a support role for a maintenance shop in Tucson. The lead man asked if there were any questions. One of the technicians raised his hand, "yeah, can we cancel this f***ing meeting?"

Apparently the lead man didn't hear him and concluded the meeting. The employee shook his head and went off into his workstation. I knew that I couldn't stay silent, and that feeling started to set in. I had only been in the company a few months and I was not in a formal leadership position, but if I remained silent, I would tacitly be endorsing the behavior since I was standing right next to this employee when he said it.

I took a few moments to gather my thoughts, then went to have a conversation with the employee. I explained to him the importance of the meeting. I told him that his behavior was disrespectful and unacceptable. I also let him know that it didn't reflect well on him as an individual; he was not acting as a leader. He did not take it well, and his body language screamed "leave me alone". I left him with my thoughts and went away.

Months later I found out that this was a turning point in my relationship with this employee. I was sitting in my boss' office with this employee when he said, "I'll happily work for Louis. He was the only one who had the guts and come tell me I was wrong to my face." All the while I thought I had damaged the relationship, when in reality, I had made it stronger.

You will face difficult circumstances and that fear is going to set in. When you feel it, instead of avoiding action, use it as a primer to remind you that now is the time to move forward!

Take Action:

What is something that instills fear in you at work? Maybe it's making calls, or even answering the phone. Maybe it's presenting publicly. Find one thing that you are apprehensive about doing, and plan on doing it once a month. Yes, actually do it once a month (at a minimum). Slowly you will notice that fear start to dissipate. You will also begin to train yourself to act when you feel that familiar tinge in your stomach.

9. The little things matter

Fort Benning, 2005

It was the last week of Airborne school also known as Jump week. Finally, after two weeks of running, falling, and instruction, we were preparing to actually jump from a "perfectly" good aircraft for the first time. We had drilled and drilled every action that we were going to undertake both inside of the aircraft and once we jumped. Randomly instructors would yell out "JUMPERS HIT IT!" and we had to perform our actions starting from the exit of the plane:

Jump forward
Good body position
Hands holding the reserve, chin down, knees together, eyes open
Count- One thousand, Two Thousand, Three thousand, four thousand
Check canopy and gain canopy control

Occasionally they would yell out some issue or failure mode and we would have to respond accordingly by pulling the reserve, avoiding another jumper, preparing for a tree landing, etc. The point was to exercise repetition to the point where the actions were second nature and muscle memory took over.

We were shuttled to the holding area where our parachutes were issued. Inside a large hangar type building were very deep benches designed specifically to hold you with a parachute on your back. It was uncomfortable to try and find a seated position before we got our chutes, and the issue process took what seemed like hours.

I finally got my parachute and started to put it on in front of the bench. By this point, we had been instructed clearly on how to do it, so it went on like a breeze. I sat down and waited once more. We had to receive an inspection before we would be clear to go to the plane. This inspection is called the Jumpmaster Personnel Inspection or JMPI. It is a detailed and rigorous check that is done for every paratrooper before boarding the plane.

I watched as the jumpmasters inspected each paratrooper. Each inspection was identical, their moves and instructions were perfectly rehearsed. Every minute detail was observed as the jumpmaster touched nearly every exposed edge of the parachute looking for any defect that could put a jumper's life in danger. It was a beautiful dance, and soldier after solder received the same exact detailed inspection.

At no point did the jumpmasters get tired (although nearly all of them had broken a sweat by the end), nor did they cut a corner. They demanded perfection at every moment, in every way, for every soldier. The stakes were too high.

Watching these instructors cycle through several hundred paratroopers with perfection was something I reflected on a week later when I was on my way to Fort Bragg to start my career as an Airborne Infantry Platoon Leader. At the time I was getting the inspection, the only thought going through my mind was, "What in the hell am I doing," but after the fear of jumping had worn off, my mind started to settle on how I was going to be a successful leader. The image of the perfect dance came to my mind. These leaders took every moment seriously. They did not slack off, they did not take a break, they did not cut a corner; they expected a flawless performance every single time.

I started to think about all the years of training I had up to that point and what it would take to execute everything I did as a leader with that same level of precision. There were too many variables in leadership to expect a perfect performance in every way, but I could still push myself to take even the smallest tasks with the utmost seriousness, execute them perfectly, then get close with the more difficult stuff.

This approach to leadership allowed me to rise to the top amongst my peers despite not being the fastest, strongest, nor smartest. It allowed me to push myself harder and farther, and it gave me the confidence to really stand out as a leader.

So here's how it works…

First, you need to decide that you will be perfect at every empirical task that can be clearly defined and has a definite measurement. For instance, if the dress code at your work is business casual, then you will be perfectly dressed with a tucked in shirt and slacks every single day (ladies, I have to be honest, I have no earthly idea what business casual is for you). Another example might be that you have to review your employee time cards once a day or once a week. Make sure it is done, on time, exactly right, every time.

You need to take some time and identify what those tasks are. If you are not currently in a leadership position, then understanding this principle and executing to it will rapidly make you one of the top individual contributors in your organization, I guarantee it.

Personal Presentation

I've already mentioned the dress code, but it's worth mentioning one more time. I want you to go to work tomorrow and look around. I'm certain there will be at least one person there who is pushing the line of acceptability of their uniform. Maybe their beard or hair is unkempt. Maybe they have their shirt untucked. Maybe they haven't cleaned their clothes appropriately. Maybe they are wearing jewelry when they shouldn't be, or don't have all the required personal protective equipment. I could think of and list any number of ways that I have seen people toe the line of acceptability. Rarely do these people get corrected for their appearance. Often they assume silence on the part of leadership is consent.

Let me tell you that as a leader of leaders, I am always looking for the next group of leaders in my organization. ALWAYS. If I am not focused on a specific task, my mind is thinking and observing the people in my organization, trying to identify the next up and comers. Personal presentation is a major factor in determining the overall character of a person. If they have the discipline to dress exactly right every single day, they have passed the first (and easiest) test of leadership aptitude. Frankly, it's a minimum standard, and yet an overwhelming amount of people fail to achieve it.

Punctuality

Another small thing you can do perfectly is show up on time every single day. Honestly, I have no idea why this is so hard for some people. I recently was interviewing a candidate who showed up 10 minutes late for his interview. He was recommended by one of my stronger employees, so before the interview, I was already thinking of hiring him. When he showed up late, I almost cancelled the interview and sent him home. He then proceeded to tell me that it was a dream of his to come and work for our company. While I'm sure he thought that was something I would like to hear, in reality it disappointed me even more. If you were offered a chance to get your dream job, would you show up late? Imagine how late he's going to be when he knows the day isn't going to be great.

I genuinely don't understand people that are habitually late. I know there are personality tests out there that talk about the different types of people and how some are not so time sensitive blah, blah, blah. I don't believe any of that baloney. I have never seen an employee jump on their boss' desk and yell, "shove it up your ass," but I have known plenty that wanted to. If you can control your behavior when it comes to how you talk to people in the workplace, you can control your schedule and show up on time.

One of the biggest ironies I find is how little patience those that are perpetually late have with others. Find these people and look at how they get frustrated when there are long lines at the grocery store or when their food takes too long to show up at a restaurant. They obviously understand the value of their own time, but clearly they don't value yours. Also, they usually are very punctual when it comes to the end of their shift.

Punctuality means more than just clocking in at the appointed hour. If you're walking through the door when your shift is supposed to begin, but aren't ready to start working until 10 to 15 minutes later, then you are still late. Punctuality also means that you show up to meetings on time, that you get your work done and turned in on time, and that you meet the commitments you have given to other people. Even simple things like when you tell someone you will get back to them by a certain time, make sure you follow through. Being punctual is an easy thing to do, but you have to want to do it.

Perfect Documents

When I deployed to Iraq I was moved to a staff position and my life consisted of sitting behind a computer in the desert, rarely getting out to fight the enemy. It was a drastic difference from my time along the Wild West border in Afghanistan. I regularly had to attend meetings at the brigade staff presentation room which built like a small movie theater. Two large canvases were along the front wall, each probably about 10 square feet. In front were rows of tables and computers with each subsequent row raised a few feet above the next. This allowed for nearly a hundred people with laptops to all watch a presentation without being obstructed.

I often stood in the back and tried to absorb the information that was relevant to my unit. I remember one day standing with a buddy of mine whispering about something not relevant to the presentation when we were interrupted by the Command Sergeant Major's (CSM) booming voice "go back!" We both looked up at the screens to see what the CSM was talking about.

"Go Forward"

"Go back"
"Go forward"
"Go back"
"Do you see it?"

The slideshows in the 82nd Airborne have a standard format that requires two insignias on every slide. On the top of one corner the 82nd Airborne insignia and on the opposing corner, the insignia for the unit. The CSM had noticed that in the transition from one slide to the next, the insignias moved, so they weren't in the exact same spot from slide to slide.

My buddy looked at me, "that's such a stupid thing for him to bitch about." I nodded in agreement, but in the back of my mind, I understood what the highest ranking enlisted member of our unit was trying to teach everyone in the room: The small things matter. Much like the jumpmasters who require perfection in every action of their inspection, we needed to treat the small things with utmost respect, especially in a place like Iraq.

My work was a reflection of myself, and while the content of a presentation is really the most important part, the details will absolutely make a difference. I learned how to use the slide master option and make sure that all my work was perfectly presented. Today I still check every slide to make sure the fonts are the same, the bullets are in the same position, the titles are the same size, and I am using the correct company formats. This isn't hard to do, and it shows you have a polished presentation.

Consider your presentations like an interview for a job. What you say in the interview matters most, but if you show up in shorts and sandals, 10 minutes late, your content is irrelevant. You have to dress appropriately, show up on time, or early, and be prepared to discuss your content. Your presentations need to be the same. In fact, ALL your work needs to be this way.

Everything you turn in is a representation of yourself and your work ethic. Keep it refined and polished! Take the extra couple minutes to read what you have written to make sure there are no misspellings and it's in the correct format. This is a simple thing to do which should take you no more than 1 minute per slide but will bear great dividends in how people perceive you as a leader.

The good part about shooting for perfection is that when you miss, you'll miss small. If you don't shoot for perfect, your misses will be much bigger.

Keep your area clean

Being clean and organized is a necessity if you want to be seen as a leader. Not only does cleanliness help keep your mind decluttered and improve your ability to focus, but it also is seen by those around you as a trait that signifies responsibility.

From the military to manufacturing, cleanliness of the work area is absolutely essential. It instills discipline and it's also the key to a safe work environment where hazards can be controlled.

I once worked at a large office that was basically a cubicle farm. In the far corner, near the bathrooms, two middle managers shared a cubicle space. I had to speak to one, and as I entered their cubicle space, I noticed the other was absent and I plopped down in her chair to have my discussion. Out of the corner of my eye, I spotted a can of soda on the desk. I turned and immediately jumped out of the chair. The desk was truly disgusting, numerous old soda cans, a half-eaten candy bar, some sort of food wrapped in a napkin, and a plethora of used napkins shoved underneath the monitor of her computer.

The guy who shared the cubicle just laughed, "yeah, everybody does that."

If everyone is grossed out by your area, how are you going to have meaningful conversations? People won't be conversing with you, they will be looking for the quickest escape. If you have to bring customers around, it's unlikely you will make the sale. If you have to counsel someone to correct behavior, they probably won't take you seriously. If you are being looked at as a future leader, and senior managers see that, it is seen as an indicator of how you will treat the business…with apathy and disrespect.

Do what you said you would

If you want to lose clout quickly, fail to respond to a request, or don't follow up when you said you would. As a leader, I get bombarded with requests multiple times a day, anything from checking on a piece of equipment, to following up on a pay issue, to any number of random ideas that one of my employees may have come up with. It is absolutely my responsibility to follow up on every single one.

I never leave my desk without something to write with. Some people have excellent memories and don't need to, but I am not that guy. The key thing for you as a leader is that these people are taking their time to talk to you about something that is important to them. If you treat it with the same level of importance, you are signaling to your employees, peers, and superiors, that you think they are important as well.

Every request requires some sort of action. Sometimes, I push things back on the employee, giving them some resources and asking them to do the research then following up on what they found. Sometimes I can quickly answer a request right on the spot. Sometimes I need to put a calendar reminder for myself weeks in the future so I don't forget. Sometimes I have to tell people to ask me again in the future when it's more relevant. But never, never, do I blow anyone off. There are many different ways to deal with a request, but no matter what you do, you HAVE to deal with the request.

Every one of us has worked with a peer or a boss that we had to ask multiple times to look into something before they did it. I want you to think back to that person in your life. How did they make you feel? Did you feel like they respected your ideas, or even you? Was that someone you wanted to follow? Now look back at your day to day. Are you being the same way towards anyone? Maybe you thought of someone, but you justified it in your mind because that person sucks somehow. They are lazy, their work is terrible, they are abrasive, whatever reason you have used to justify the way you treat that person, let me tell you it's time for you to change your behavior.

Why, you ask?

Because everyone is watching you always.

That's right, when you rolled your eyes at the janitor who needed to get around you, people noticed. When you ignored the request of your least favorite person in the office, people noticed. When you didn't follow up for the third time this month, people noticed.

True leaders rise above the fray, they don't play favorites, and they live it by treating every person, and every idea, the same.

I know what you're thinking, "he doesn't know MY situation." You're right, I don't know your situation, but if you're treating some people like they are less important, I can tell you you're wrong, and you're not built for leadership. It may be harsh, but until you're ready to act mature and treat people and their ideas equally, no matter how they have treated you, you will never truly be a leader.

Workplace Gossip

It's easy to get sucked into workplace gossiping. As much as I hate to admit it, even I have been sucked in a time or two. When you are a leader, people will talk to you, and you are going to hear some serious behind the curtain type information. It's going to be up to you not to indulge these conversations. If someone wants to tell you about themselves, fine, but if they want to tell you about someone else in a way that isn't helpful, cut that conversation short.

I recently had a sidebar conversation with a few of my subordinate leaders. I heard that there were rumblings about how much certain people were getting paid and two informal leaders were involved in the conversation. This seemed pretty out of character for these two, but I used it as an opportunity to re-engage them on the importance of professional conduct.

As a leader, I'm always looking at the short list of guys that I think are going to lead the next generation. These two were on my short list, but if they were going to be sowing the seeds of discontent inside the workplace, then they didn't have what it took to be leaders. Especially since they were encouraging or at the very least, allowing employees to criticize one another in a non-fruitful way.

I used the opportunity to talk about the company's pay structure and what each of them could do to get to the next level. I also showed them how they could have the same conversation with their peers. Whether or not they had actually been complaining wasn't confirmed, but my message about how they should conduct themselves was very well taken. I later received a report from their leader that these guys were pumped and pushing harder with great attitudes.

What I want you to take away is that your leaders, two or three levels up, are constantly looking at the next generation. Had I not gone and talked to these guys, I may have moved them down on my list. If you are a person who loves gossip and talking about other people, everyone is going to know. They will start to think, "if that's what he says about so-and-so, what does he say about me when I'm not around?" Your senior leaders are going to start discounting you as a potential up and comer. Finally, it's just an asshole thing to do. Seriously, no one wants to follow a gossip, just don't engage in it.

Take Action:
There are several examples in this chapter of areas where we tend to slip: Dress code, details, gossip, etc. Pick one, and for the next few months, keep working on it until you have mastered it. When it becomes a habit (like keeping your shirt tucked in at all times) and NOT doing it feels awkward, pick another and work on that. Make perfection a habit!

10. Dealing with Failure

Fort Bragg, 2008

Sometime early in my deployment to Iraq I decided that I wanted to be a Green Beret. My best friend had made it through the selection gauntlet and was half-way into his Qualification Course. I also made friends with a long-tabber (a name given to guys who earned the Special Forces tab) that was in my unit in Iraq, and between the both of them, I decided that I didn't want to become an intelligence officer and instead wanted to continue to be a combat leader in the US Army Special Forces.

I trained every single day for 13 months in Iraq. I pushed my body to new limits, shredding the fat and toning the muscle. I ran the Army 10 miler in 67 minutes, I could do over 100 push-ups without rest, and I got bored with sit-ups long before I got tired. I could run a 10 minute mile pace with a 60 pound ruck on my back. I was in the best shape of my life. By the time I started the Special Forces Assessment and Selection course (SFAS), I was a senior Lieutenant with 24 months of combat experience and in prime physical shape. I was as ready as anyone could be.

As the course started, I was confident and comfortable. The course pushed me to my limits in just a matter of hours, but I had trained for this and was mentally ready to push on. As the days progressed, my confidence only grew. I was quickly rising as a strong leader of my squad, and I was motivated to continue.

We arrived at the obstacle course, usually my worst event. Over my entire army career, I struggled to negotiate obstacles. One because I'm afraid of heights, but mostly because I'm so damn short. The instructor yelled "go" and off I went. The first few I negotiated flawlessly, boosting my confidence even further. I was feeling pumped because I had never done so well in an obstacle course before. My year of preparation had paid off.

I got to this particular obstacle which was a large rope that attached to a log that led to some monkey bars. You had to climb the rope, slide down the log, then walk across the top of the monkey bars. I climbed the rope without a problem, slid down the log, and started to walk on the monkey bars. As I stepped forward, my left leg started to shake. I stepped back, shimmied in place, shrugged it off and stepped forward with purpose.

snap

The sound reminded me of snapping a handful of carrots in half. My knee buckled and I fell onto the monkey bars, catching myself before hitting the ground. A sharp pain surged up my leg and I looked down. My leg was sideways and my kneecap was on the side of my leg. I reached down, put my kneecap back in place, and sat for a moment to catch my breath.

"Candidate! You have failed to negotiate the obstacle. Get off my obstacle!"

The instructor must have heard the loud snap, but his current job was not to take care of my medical needs, it was to weed out the men who didn't have what it took to become Green Berets.

I dropped off the monkey bars, careful not to land on my left leg. I limped over to the instructor, who in a matter of fact tone noted, "Candidate, you have failed to negotiate the obstacle, would you like to try again?"

"Um…yeah, but can I see a medic?"

"Sure, if you quit. Do you quit?"

I didn't train for over a year to quit now. I had never quit anything in my life, and I was not about to start now.

"No. I don't quit. I'll try again."

I got back in line and tried to run in place with the other candidates. My leg was incredibly unstable. I could barely stand, let alone run in place. I could feel my kneecap moving and the pain was gut wrenching. I kept going, I wasn't about to quit.

It was finally my turn again. I tried to climb the rope, but I couldn't put weight on my leg, so I climbed only using the power of my arms. When I got to the top, I locked out my leg to throw it over the log, and in that instant, my kneecap came out a second time. This time the pain was even more intense than the first time. I was high enough that I couldn't let go of the rope without falling and incurring significantly more injuries. I wrapped my good leg around the rope, held on with one arm, and put the kneecap back with my other arm, barely holding the rope as I slid quickly to the ground. I hit the ground with a thud, holding my knee and wincing in pain.

This time the instructor said nothing (or he may have but I was in too much pain to hear it). I slowly stood up and limped over to him. "I need to see a medic," the words came out softly. He looked at me emotionless, "Do you quit?" My eyes met his, I looked down at my knee and back at him. As a knot formed in my throat, "Yes. I quit."

I made my way over to the medics and eventually to the small clinic on site. By then, my knee was quite swollen, and bruising had developed. The doctor there could tell I was really distraught as he was looking my knee over. "It's ok, you'll be a medical drop and you can come back again in the future when you heal." I looked at him, "actually I can't. I'm already a senior 1st Lieutenant. This was my only shot." We both got quiet as that sentence settled in the room.

This was the first time I ever really failed at anything. I completely and utterly failed. There was no redo, no other chance to go back. That was it. The dream was over in an instant.

When I look back at this, even as I write it now, a smile comes over my face. First, I learned how to deal with failure. Second, I learned that sometimes failure is our greatest gift. Because I dislocated my knee, I was sent to Fort Huachuca, Arizona to become an intelligence officer. While there I met my wife, and today I am blessed with three beautiful children and a wonderful and fulfilling marriage.

Sometimes as leaders, we aren't going to meet our goals. Our teams are going to fail. It will happen. It's up to us to learn the lessons from those failures, but more importantly not to dwell on them. I had a new career as an intelligence officer, and since I am committed to excellence, I did not have time to feel sorry for myself. I had to learn to become the best intelligence officer that I could. I also would soon have the added responsibility of learning to be a husband and a father.

A missed goal is not something to dwell on. It's an opportunity to find new goals and work to achieve them. Learn whatever lessons you can and move forward. My identity and success were not predicated on becoming a green beret, but I didn't learn that lesson until the dream of becoming one was gone.

Years later, my knee still gives me problems, and the doctors tell me that arthritis is pretty much a guarantee. I've dislocated it a couple more times since then and have had multiple surgeries. I get reminded of my failure pretty much every time I go up a staircase or run a couple miles, but then I think of my family and the drastic change of course my life has taken thanks to that injury.

It's ok to fail sometimes. Learn from it, set new goals, and then crush those.

Take action:
What is one thing that you have failed at? How did it make you feel? How did it affect your confidence? What did it make you think about yourself? Take a moment and write it down. Now, when you have made a list of the ways that failure affected the way you think about yourself, list out the ways that is wrong. For example, failing in Special Forces made me feel like I wasn't a great soldier, but going

back and thinking about the ways I had succeeded as a warrior helped me realize that a single event did not define who I was. We tend to focus on the negative, take the time to highlight your wins!

Keep On Leading Yourself: A Summary

I strongly believe that leadership is an art form, and like any art, there is an element of natural talent. While leaders can come in many forms, some people are definitely more poised for the art. That being said, Leadership can be taught! In order to learn, however, you need to be in the right state. I have spent over 15,000 words just talking about how you need to change and lead yourself, before discussing anything about how we can use leadership to grow the bottom line of your business. The point is that you need to look to yourself first before you start thinking about leadership.

Honor, integrity, initiative, attitude, punctuality, cleanliness, discipline, the list of leadership characteristics are nearly all completely in your control. These are principles by which you need to live. Let me emphasize this, you need to *live* by those principles, you can't just practice them for a few hours a day when you're in the office. Deciding to be a leader is a total commitment to a lifestyle that will govern your every move.

You cannot "fake it 'til you make it" when it comes to leadership. People will eventually see through the charade and stop following you. If your personal life is in shambles, your work life will soon follow. If you are going to become irreplaceable in the workplace, you need to be able to focus 100% on what you are doing while you're there. A person with strife at home will struggle to stay on point at work.

This is something that no one in the $14 Billion leadership training market will tell you, because in the 21st century we really love easy solutions. Directors want to see a program that they can implement that has clear, objective criteria that can be applied to every circumstance, and they are told that this new "method" is the key to leadership. That's not how people work, and that's not how leadership works.

You cannot follow a 5-step conversation format when you're disciplining someone and think that this somehow is going to make up for all the months and years of terrible leadership you've given them to this point. The people in your organization that succeed with those tools are those that are already successful leaders. They can take elements from whatever training program you give them, find what is useful and meets their style, and then implement it. They have already committed to leading themselves and their teams respect them for it.

Real leadership, the kind of leadership that results in measurable positive change in an organization, *that* takes work and commitment on the part of the individual who wants to lead. Much like the alcoholic or addict who decides to become sober, or the entrepreneur who starts a business, or the woman who becomes a mother, these are major life changes and not part-time endeavors. Leadership is the same. If you decide and commit to be a leader, then you need to get ready to change your life.

First, you lead yourself, then you can begin to lead your people.

<u>KEEP ON LEADING PEOPLE</u>

Introduction

Afghanistan, 2005

I consider myself extremely blessed and lucky to have had the opportunity to lead men in the illustrious 82nd Airborne division as an airborne infantry officer, particularly in the challenging and extreme environment that was our deployment to the Afghan mountains. Much of the leadership lessons I impart today were learned through the rigors of combat, deep on the front lines alongside some of the bravest Americans anyone could ever hope to meet. It was there that I learned the power of relationships when it comes to leadership.

After the major firefight I discussed in the beginning of this book (where a large enemy force managed to surround my element and injure one of my soldiers), Captain Teague decided to take a large contingent of US and Afghan soldiers back to the mountaintop where our fight had occurred; hilltop 2911. It was strategic terrain, over 10,000 feet high with great visibility of much of our area of operation and sat right on the border with Pakistan. Access to the mountaintop from the Pakistan side was relatively easy, whereas the Afghan side of the mountain was rougher terrain and a treacherous road. This provided the enemy a great opportunity to enter into Afghanistan, attack, and ex-filtrate quickly.

Teague stopped by the small outpost where my squad of nine men was stationed as a border checkpoint. We were regularly hammered by rockets from 2911, and we could see the summit as he briefed me about his plan. Nearly 100 US and Afghan forces were going to assault the mountain with artillery, mortar, and air support. They anticipated a large fight.

We stood next to his vehicle with a map laid out on the hood of his truck, getting a briefing on the battle plan. My small contingent would remain in support, only to be called upon if the battle got particularly difficult. "Sir, we know the terrain, and my guys are itching to take it to the enemy after they overwhelmed us yesterday," my squad leader chimed in. I agreed and continued to push for a more active involvement in the fight. Our tenacity did not go unnoticed, but the leader's decision at that time was that we would remain in the rear and wait to be called upon if needed.

We watched as the large convoy took off towards the mountaintop and began briefing our small force of the plan. The men were eager to get back into the fight, and all checked and re-checked their equipment sitting in silence waiting for the radio to chirp so we could move out. Hours passed as we watched and waited, then finally the call came.

"Bravo36 this is Bravo6, come in over"

The men lit up, Teague was calling for me. I grabbed the hand mic and responded, "this is bravo36, go ahead over."

"We have reports of a large enemy force massing for an attack. Grab your unit and meet at the following grid coordinates…" Before I had the grid coordinates copied down, the men were already moving, and in seconds all nine of them had piled into two trucks and the vehicles were running.

We blazed through the mountain dirt roads and arrived in less than an hour to a small clearing at the base of the mountain that was being used as a forward command post. I hopped out of my vehicle and made my way to Captain Teague who was coordinating all the units. He stepped out of his vehicle and met me.

"There's 40-60 enemy massing on the hilltop. I have 1st Platoon and the Afghan Platoon on this hill in a blocking position," He pointed to a ridgeline that shot off the hilltop where the bulk of our forces were positioned. "I need you to take your element and clear the hilltop towards 1st platoon."

My eyebrows shot up in disbelief, "sir, I only have nine men." He responded, "I know. You will also have the 120mm mortar support, and the Apaches are already enroute." I smiled and jokingly answered, "Aren't WE supposed to outnumber them 3 to 1 instead of the other way around?" He smiled back, "you have plenty of combat multipliers Louis." "Roger that sir," I responded quickly and made my way to my men who were sitting eagerly in the trucks waiting for their mission.

My squad leader met me mid-way, "So what's the plan?"

"There's 40-60 guys up there, we're going up and clearing the mountain."

"WHAT?! Are you serious?"

"Yep, we will have the mortars and Apaches are on their way"

"Does he realize there's only nine of us?"

"Yep"

"What's 1st platoon doing?"

"They're in a blocking position over there."

"Roger that"

He smiled big enough to show his teeth and chuckled, then shook his head and made his way to the rest of the group. He approached the team and a similar conversation took place.

"Alright men, there's about 40-60 enemy on the hilltop, we're going up." The response was a cacophony of disbelief. Several asked what 1st Platoon was doing. "1st Platoon is in a blocking position over there… Look, all I have to say is I have some letters and addresses on the board in my hooch. You have 5 minutes before we go." The men began to laugh, and a few lit up a final cigarette.

Teague walked up to me as I watched them prepare to move, "You really think they should be smoking cigarettes before you scale a 10,000 foot mountain?" I turned to him, "Really sir?" He smiled once again and threw his hands up as he backed away.

I looked at my men and felt a surge of emotion mixed with pride, fear, excitement, disbelief, and awe. I was reminded of the story of the Spartan 300 at Thermopylae.

While many of the details of the ancient tale are surely mired with embellishments, the story is that 300 Spartan men went off to fight the largest army ever assembled by that point in history. King Darius was defeated by the Greeks in the battle of Marathon, and his son Xerxes vowed to return to Greece and seek his revenge. He spent years amassing this incredible force and invaded Greece by both land and sea.

The Athenians asked the Spartans to assist them in the defense of Greece, but a religious festival prevented the Spartans from sending their full army forth. Their King Leonidas visited the oracle at Delphi who told him, "In order for Greece to survive, a Spartan King must die." Leonidas went back to Sparta and took 300 men with him to fight the Persians. He required that every man that came with him had a son. He placed his force of 300 (and a couple thousand other Greeks) in a small pass called Thermopylae. It was bordered by a mountain on one side and the Mediterranean Sea on the other. This would effectively limit the Persian Army's ability to mass their full numbers in the attack and would have to come in waves instead.

King Xerxes sent his spies to go and see what the Greeks were doing in preparation for battle. The spies were in disbelief when they saw the Spartans. These men were preparing to face off with a Persian army of tens of thousands, and the Spartans were laughing and joking with each other as they prepared for battle; not a tinge of fear could be felt in the group.

I remember the first time I read the story I thought these men were so calm from having been trained since childhood for such a battle, but now, experiencing it myself, I realized that this confidence for battle ran much deeper than training; it was because of their relationship with each other. It was through our relationships that we earned complete and implicit trust and confidence in each other.

We loved each other like family and were prepared to face death with one another.

This was a lesson I will never forget. Captain Teague had earned my trust through his outstanding leadership, and so I was able to give an order to assault up a 10,000 foot mountain against an enemy in fortified positions, more than three times our size...and I did it with a smile. My men also smiled. Had there been enemy spies, they would have seen men laughing and joking with each other, smoking cigarettes, and preparing themselves and their equipment for battle without any fear whatsoever.

While the spy may be able to see the outward manifestation of excellent leadership, what he would have missed is the work put into building such a relationship with a team. This is not something that can only be done inside of the context of combat, it's something any leader can apply. Do this and your subordinates will follow you wherever you take them.

This second section of the book deals with how to build those relationships. How you can get to know your people and lead them as individuals. Often as leaders our intent and focus is to move the team in a certain direction. Budgets, deadlines, expenses, profit, all those are measured by team results, and therefore it's reasonable to try and move the team to meet key performance metrics. The problem with that approach is that your team is not an entity in and of itself. Your team is composed of individuals, and influencing and moving those individuals is a delicate dance that can only be coordinated once you can lead every member of the group individually.

11. Get to know your people

I took over a team whose morale was extremely low. Productivity was lagging behind, our ability to complete jobs inside the quoted timelines seemed impossible. Safety was more of a lip-service type operation at the lowest levels than an actual culture of action. The shop was poorly maintained, cluttered, and devoid of cleanliness. Promotions and training opportunities that the company had were not being disseminated to the team, and we were starting to see good people leave our organization. I had to take action fast.

The team was about 25 people with three leaders that reported directly to me. I joked with my wife that I was a platoon leader again for the third time. Her witty response came instantly, "you better know what the hell you're doing then."

My first act was to set a standard of guiding leadership principles for my leaders. I sat them down in a private room and walked them through my expectations. Below is a copy of that document:

The following is a list of my leadership principles. This is not a comprehensive list, as I'm sure something has been forgotten, but it serves as a cornerstone of key elements that I will follow and expect you to follow as well. In the end, without follow through, these are just words and empty promises, it is our job to follow through and make them reality.

In no particular order:
1. Leadership is a responsibility
2. Leadership is service *before* authority
3. Our actions are more important than our words
4. I will never compromise safety. This is absolutely non-negotiable
5. Set the example, for instance:
   a. Give respect before expecting it
   b. Never compromise your principles
   c. Always act with the utmost integrity
   d. If you don't want anyone to know about it, then you probably shouldn't be doing it
   e. Always wear the proper PPE
   f. Never ask someone else to do something if you can do it
   g. Never walk by trash
6. Always place people first
   a. No unsafe acts
   b. Never walk by an unsafe act
   c. No unrealistic requests
   d. No surprises in evaluations
   e. Recognize exemplary behavior
   f. Praise in public, correct in private
   g. Get to know the career goals of all your employees and have an action plan to get there
   h. Inconvenience yourself before your employees
7. Open communication is critical
   a. Bad news doesn't get better with time. The sooner you tell me about a problem, the sooner I can help
   b. If I make an unreasonable request, let me know
   c. If I present a problem I will either present a solution, or make it abundantly clear that I'm looking for options; I expect you to do the same
   d. Instead of talking about why we can't accomplish a goal, we will talk about how we could accomplish that goal

    e. I will not withhold important information that
       you need to do your job
  8. I will talk about failures in the context of what *I*
     could have done, and what organizational changes we
     need to make before assigning any sort of blame to
     anyone but **myself**.

I am not infallible, I will make mistakes. I promise to own
those mistakes and apologize. I will never ask you or anyone
else to do something I myself wouldn't do. I am hereby
giving you the express authority to correct me if I fail in
any of the above.

We belabored over each point. We discussed what our failings had been in the past as a team, and what we would do moving forward. Step one complete.

Step two was to take action. Our immediate short-term actions were to start instilling discipline in the team and showing concern on our part as leaders. I showed up on a Saturday, got on my hands and knees, and helped clean up the shop.

The next act was to correct any evaluations that had lagged behind. At this employer, every year, each employee received a yearly evaluation on their hiring anniversary. That evaluation directly impacted what their raise would be. A late evaluation meant that employees wouldn't get their raise in time. Eventually, when it was completed, they would get back pay as a bonus, but that comes at a bigger tax burden. So by not getting paperwork done on time, we were actually impacting employee pay.

I clearly explained to my leaders that any outstanding evaluations had to be completed immediately. I further told them if they were responsible for a late evaluation, they would be receiving a written warning. Any employee with a written warning was not eligible for a raise for a year. Therefore, if they didn't make the time for their employees, they would personally forfeit their own raise for the year. If it happened multiple times, they would lose their job.

In addition to cleaning up paperwork, I told them I expected them to do monthly one on one conversations with every one of their direct reports. Each of them had about 8 guys, so two hours a week would need to be dedicated to completing one on ones.

Immediately I was confronted with the all too familiar complaint: "I don't have time." I was not going to accept this excuse. "Not true," I told them, "You *do* have time, you just haven't made it a priority. I don't have time in my schedule to go to the hospital right now, but if this phone rings and one of my kids is there, I all of a sudden have time for the hospital. Why? Because it became a priority over everything else. Don't lie and say you don't have time, say you haven't made it a priority. If you can say 'I haven't made it a priority' without being embarrassed, then you're ok, but if you're embarrassed to tell someone you haven't made it a priority, then you should make it a priority."

I gave them this example, say someone told me to watch a particular movie and then followed up with me a week later to see if I had watched it. I would not be embarrassed to say, "I haven't made it a priority." If instead someone asked me if I finished their yearly evaluation, I would be mortified to tell them that I haven't made it a priority, therefore I need to properly prioritize my work. "When your employees see that you have made them a priority," I explained, "then they will respond with effort and make *your* requests a priority as well."

Dear reader, if you are not doing one on ones with your direct reports, you need to start immediately. There is almost no better tool in the leader toolbox to influence your team and change a culture than the one on one conversation.

First, let me explain briefly what a one on one is not:

- It is not a report of current tasks and projects with your employees.
- It is not a sidebar conversation or "check-in" at their work area
- An open-door policy does not count

I had a boss that used scheduled one on ones as a time to update her on all of my projects. I was already doing regular updates, so this just became yet another task on my part to prepare an update; it was a waste of time for both of us. I've also seen leaders who walk up to employees while they are working and chat for a couple minutes thinking they have completed their one on one requirement...they haven't. Finally, I've seen leaders, senior leaders in particular who say they have an open-door policy, "they can come see me whenever they want!" Yeah, no. Not the same.

A one on one is an opportunity for a leader to really get to know their direct reports. Not on a superficial level, but on a much deeper level. Use the opportunity to learn what motivates your employees, how they like to be recognized, what they like about their job, what they don't like, what they want to do in the future, how they think their job can be improved, what problems they are experiencing, and more. As a leader you should be asking questions and doing very little talking. Tell your employees that you are giving them an hour of your time every month for them to talk about whatever they want.

It took a little while for everyone to get used to the new modus operandi. In the beginning, my employees were uncomfortable in the one on one conversation, and we spent a lot of time discussing what conversations topics should be. Their answers were short and to the point, and they were just ready to get out of there. Before I started, getting called into the boss' office always spelled bad news. After a couple months, however, the conversations evolved, and my guys began to look forward to the conversations. They started to open up about the real troubles they were facing, what motivated them, their family life, and what their long term hopes and dreams were. All of our relationships grew much stronger in a very short time. Thanks to these conversations, I was able to start developing career paths for each guy and set them on a track that suited each individual. Morale spiked.

More than the improvement in morale was that my ability to have tough conversations about performance issues was greatly improved. Because I had already established a relationship where I had proven through my actions that I genuinely cared about each individual on the team, when I told them I was disappointed, it mattered to them. When I told them their actions were harming the team, they changed their behaviors. When I told them they had more potential than they were living up to, they knew I was right.

In addition, I received a lot of personal feedback that was greatly beneficial. My employees were open about what I was doing well, what I was doing poorly, how I could communicate better with them, and what their genuine frustrations were in the job. Our company had a very detailed career roadmap for technicians, and because I had heard so many guys ask about how to get promoted and get raises, I presented them with this roadmap. Turned out that almost none of them had ever seen it. As leaders, we had not made our direct reports and their needs a priority. All these guys knew was that they were working as hard as possible, but still didn't seem to move up in the company. One guy told me, "I've basically wasted the last three years by not doing any of this." While many of them were frustrated that they had never seen it, they were motivated and excited to finally have a plan for their careers. I would never had known that this was a festering issue in my team without the one on one conversations.

Leadership requires humility, humility means you need to be willing to receive feedback from your employees. It's just as, if not MORE important, than you giving them "feedback". In those one on one conversations, your employees are giving you the inside secrets on how to best motivate and influence them. This information is invaluable if you want to meet the goals set by your superiors. It's a lot like playing a video game with a book that tells you exactly how to beat the game. If you need to quickly turn a team around and show that you genuinely care about each member of the team, start the one on ones. After two or three, your team will start to realize that this isn't some sort of fad, but an honest effort to learn about and act on *their* needs and wants, and they will move mountains for you in return.

This tool is virtually foolproof if you have already led yourself as described in the beginning of this book. Using the one on one is a master key to leadership success that works in every environment, in every climate, in every scenario, every single time. I can tell you from almost two decades in leadership as of this writing, that while each individual is unique and you will have to tailor your conversation to each person, EVERYONE loves the opportunity to sit down with their direct supervisor and have a private, valuable, uninterrupted, safe, conversation.

Take Action:

Go ahead and schedule a recurring one on one meeting with every one of your direct reports. I recommend you do them monthly, but every other month will work (quarterly at the absolute minimum). I know you have some great excuses as to why this is inconvenient. I know it is, but it's worth it. Right now, put down this book, pull up your calendar, and schedule the meetings. If people are all over the country or world, then make them virtual. If you think you have a really compelling excuse, try me, send me an email at louis@louisjfernandez.com with the subject "why I can't do one on ones" and see if I can't bury your silly excuse.

12. Tom Brady Can't Block

The weaknesses of your employees don't matter…at least not as much as their strengths.

Whether or not you like Tom Brady, you have to recognize that he is one of the greatest football players that has ever played the sport. He has led his team from one of the worst in the NFL, to a dynasty of greatness that any non-patriots fan is tired of seeing in Super Bowls.

Imagine for a moment if his coaches had approached performance reviews in the same way that we see in the 21st century workplace. "Well Tom, you've done an excellent job this year. Our team was able to win the super bowl, but there were some missteps along the way. You did lose a few games, and you threw quite a few interceptions. I also didn't see you working on blocking at all this year. To really be a valuable player in this team, you need to be more well-rounded, and your 40 yard dash time is quite lacking. I also would like to see you spend more time with the defense and special teams so you understand better how they work. Right now, the only position you can really play is Quarterback, but we really need to make sure you can play in more positions. In addition, our offense is limited in the type of plays we can run because you're a pocket passer and can't really run the ball. We have a stretch goal of being able to run the option successfully which is going to require a lot of work on your part. So in order to achieve the top rating, you're going to have to work on some of these weaknesses to supplement your strengths."

If you were a team owner, you'd do the team well to fire that coach because he has no idea how to run that team. If Tom Brady was a good passer, a decent blocker, an average runner, could catch a ball, and was quick on his feet, he wouldn't be a *better* player, in fact, he probably wouldn't be in the NFL at all. What makes Brady great is that he is an excellent quarterback. Not only that, but he also has specialized the type of quarterback that he is. His coaches have embraced Brady's strengths and played the game based on those strengths. When Brady goes to practice, he focuses on what he is good at, ensuring he gets better at his strengths. The fact that Brady can't block is irrelevant and it would be a waste of supreme talent and potential to focus on improving his weaknesses.

I'm sure as you read this it becomes painfully obvious that in order to build a winning NFL team, you need to find people with particular strengths that are specialized in each position with a type of gameplay that compliments the rest of the team. Why then don't we do this in the workplace?

We have been conditioned through bureaucratic limitations to rate every employee on the same metrics. As leaders in the civilian world, we have been taught to provide feedback that focuses on areas of improvement, and worse, we have not been taught to recognize the value in specialization and improving strengths.

As a combat leader, I was always paying attention to what my soldiers were particularly good at. I remember distinctly in a remote border checkpoint in Afghanistan when we were conducting some "ready-up" drills. These drills are focused on training soldiers to respond quickly to targets from different firing positions. Each soldier has a unique target with circles, squares, and triangles on it. Each shape is a different color. The soldier stands with the target either in front, to a side, or behind him. The range instructor then calls out a shape or a color then yells "ready-up!" The soldier turns to face the target, looks at the 6 different colored shapes, identifies the target that corresponds, lifts the weapon, moves the selector from safe to semi, fires a controlled pair (two shots) into the target, places the weapon back on safe, and goes back into the starting position. All this happens in less than two seconds. The more you drill, the faster you become, until it all becomes muscle memory and you are able to accomplish the task without even pausing to think. This is a critical task, particularly in close combat operations when any number of targets can present themselves without warning and you have a moment in time to assess and act.

During this particular range day, there were two soldiers that had developed a healthy competition and were trying to one-up each other. Both were evenly matched, but one of these men carried a 203 grenade launcher on his weapon. At some point in the back and forth, the one who carried the grenade launcher issued a challenge. Not long after, we finished the exercise and set up a small grenade launcher range for both of them.

There was an abandoned hut about 200 yards away. On that hut was a door and a window, whichever one of them got a grenade into the window or door first would be the de-facto winner. They counted,

One…two…three…slunk, slunk, both fired at the same time. My jaw dropped when both grenades slipped through the small window and exploded inside the hut. From that day forward, both of them carried grenade launchers.

My platoon had about 35 men. Some of them were designated marksmen, some carried machine guns, and some carried grenade launchers. We had a medic, a forward observer, eight team leaders, four squad leaders, a platoon sergeant, and me. Each of us was specialized in our particular job. We trained on those jobs and focused on our skills. If a guy was an excellent marksman, but couldn't carry and maintain a machine gun, I kept him in a sharpshooter role rather than having him focus on learning the machine gun. If a guy had a great eye for spotting IED's, I kept him in the lead truck.

During one mission, I went out with a squad of guys on a patrol of the local mountains. The point man had his compass reading pointing him to our destination and followed the azimuth with complete disregard of the terrain. As we walked we went up, then down, then up, then down this brutal Afghan terrain. After just a few miles, I was starting to feel the exhaustion of traversing the terrain in my body. I called the squad to a halt and moved to the squad leader's position. "Look, this is your patrol, so I don't want to intervene, but your point man is killing me with this up and down. Look at the map," I pointed at the terrain, "this is where we are going. He either goes up and follows this ridge, or he stays in this cut and we climb one time at the end. I'm done going up and down."

The squad leader smiled, he was trying to teach a lesson on land navigation. While following the azimuth was one way of arriving to your destination, a good point man would recognize the terrain and adjust the route accordingly. This squad leader was trying to improve a weakness, and the effect was that it was hindering the team. After a couple more miles with no change, he finally made the decision to change who was running point, and it was smooth sailing after that.

That original point man was an excellent combat leader. He knew how to motivate his men, take care of them, and ensure they were ready for battle at all times. Under enemy contact, he was able to lead and maneuver appropriately. He was highly skilled in a particular area, but he was a terrible point man. Rather than try and improve his weakness, it was more beneficial to the team to allow someone else to run point, and this young combat leader to focus on his strength. In the end, our entire team was stronger and more prepared to fight when we arrived at our objective.

If you want to build stronger winning teams, you need to identify each individual's strengths and allow them work on those strengths. People are motivated by their successes. They are happier when they are doing what they are good at. Your teams are more successful and willing to take on tougher challenges when they are simply focusing on getting better at what they are already good at.

Your job as a leader should not be to improve what people are weak at, but improve what they are already good at. So instead of searching for weaknesses, search for strengths, place people in positions that compliment those strengths, and focus your training on enhancing those strengths. Soon you will find a happier, more productive workplace.

Take Action:

Make a list of everyone on your team, and next to each person's name, write one thing they are really good at. This includes the low performers. If you need help, look to other leaders that work with your team. If you struggle with this task, then you need to pay attention to the good things people are doing until you have it complete. Once that's done, then you can start giving people tasks that correspond to their strengths.

13. What if it was someone you loved?

Fort Bragg, 2006

In the 82nd Airborne every unit needs to go through a Deployment Ready Force rotation, or DRF as it is known. When a unit is on DRF, they are on a recall anywhere from 2-16 hours. That means, once you get a call, you have two hours to get to your unit, with your gear, and be ready to deploy. There are several code words that mean different things:

1. Just a phone roster check
2. You need to come in, but just for formation
3. You need to come in, but just for training
4. You're deploying somewhere

Usually, you will get a "#1" once a week, and a "#3" once during your rotation. It's not often that the DRF is called into actual combat, but it has happened in the past.

In preparation for our rotation, we had to basically prepare the unit to deploy. It meant having all our gear packed at all times, and we had to stay within one hour of travel time to the base. We couldn't

114

drink alcohol, had to keep our phones on us at all times, and we lived on alert as our company was on a two hour recall.

I awoke at 3am to the overly loud ringer on my phone. My eyes were closed as I answered. "Lieutenant Fernandez?" the voice on the phone asked. "Yes, go ahead," I was still half asleep. The voice on the other end of the line then uttered the #4 code word. I was instantly awake, my eyes opened wide and I sat up in my bed.
"Say again. Did you say #4?"
"Yes, sir #4"
"Are you sure #4?"
"Yes sir, that is what I was asked to call."
"Roger, enroute."

I hung up the phone and sprang up out of the bed. I ran to the bathroom and turned on the news on the way. I figured if the 82nd was being called to deploy somewhere, the chaos in the world would be on the news.

Nothing.

I was surprised, and as I brushed my teeth, I began to think about which possible country we'd be jumping into. Iran maybe? Somewhere in Africa? I'd be lying if I said I wasn't excited. The 82nd hadn't done a combat jump in years, and I was finally going to be part of it.

I got in my car, fully dressed, in uniform, ready to rock-and-roll. I pulled up to the unit parking lot, and all the lights were off except for my company. This didn't make sense. If we were deploying, I would expect to see the entire battalion and brigade staff buzzing, getting ready to send hundreds of warfighters and their equipment into battle.

As I parked my car, I saw one of our soldiers with his whole family in the parking lot. His little girls were crying, and his wife was wiping away tears as they gave each other a hug. They didn't know where daddy was going or how long he was going to be gone, just that he was leaving. I was single at the time, so I had no one waiting for me, but the image impacted me quite a bit. I locked my car and headed for the building.

I approached the building and there were two soldiers outside with large trash bags collecting cell phones. I walked past, with no intention of giving up mine. "Sir, you need to give up your cell phone." I was the second in command of the company, and by this point I was highly skeptical of what was going on. I could see that no one in our higher command staff was at work, and no other company had been called in. I needed my phone to figure out what the heck was going on as I planned on making some phone calls. I shook my head no, and they didn't insist. I walked straight to my commander's office without talking to anyone, although I was inundated with questions by every passing soldier.

"What's going on sir, I got a #4?" I asked as I walked into the commander's office without knocking. He looked up from his computer, "get in formation and I'll address the company when everyone is accounted for." I spun around, walked into my office, picked up my phone and started making phone calls. No one had any idea what was going on, clearly we weren't deploying; someone called the wrong code word.

I'm not sure how long it was before the formation was finally ready. We were all at the base of the headquarters ready to go when the commander finally came out. "Gentlemen, great job! In less than two hours you were able to get everyone here and in formation. Today we are going to conduct a 15 mile road march to a range, do some shooting, then you will get picked up and returned here to be released. At which point you will get your phones returned and can call your families…"

He continued talking, but at this point I was no longer listening. The first sergeant and I stood next to each other in formation. He turned to me, "Did you know about this?" I could tell in the tone of his voice that he was on the verge of rage. "I had no idea, I just got the #4." He looked at me intently and I could see the fire in his eyes as he stared deep into my soul to determine if I was lying. His expression showed he saw my sincerity and slowly diverted his angry gaze back towards the commander.

As the second in command, it was my job to ensure the soldiers had all the necessary supplies to complete their mission. The fact that the commander had organized this event meant that I had no idea if anything had been arranged. As soon as the company was dismissed to prepare to step off on their march, I approached the commander. "Sir, did you get everything set up? Do you have ammo, water, a trail vehicle, the range, etc?" He looked at me and smirked, "I got the range, you got a few hours to organize the rest."

I was furious. What he had just asked me to do was a near impossible task. All of these supplies had to be requested, often weeks in advance. In order to make this happen, I would have to get extremely creative, and even grey some lines that shouldn't be grey.

As I scurried to make things happen, the image of that family in the parking lot kept rolling through my brain like a slideshow on loop.

Eventually the exercise ended. The soldiers got the food, water, and ammunition they needed, and at the end of the day they were able to call their families to say they weren't actually deploying. My commander and I also got into a very "spirited" debate on what was appropriate. Tempers flared, and I'm ashamed to admit I lost my professional bearing. Eventually I was reassigned to another unit right before we deployed, but I learned an invaluable lesson that day:

Every person that works for you is the most important person in the world to someone. Respect that.

Each of us is someone's child, or husband, or wife, or nephew, or cousin, or lover, whatever. There is someone in this world that loves you more than anything else. The same is true for each of your employees. Every decision you make as a leader is going to affect the most important person in the world to someone.

So now I ask you this question: Would you be willing to look that loved one in the eye and defend your actions?

Asking the question a different way: Would you be proud to have your child on your team? Would you want them treated the way you are treating your employees?

That day I was embarrassed of my command, and my soldiers could not believe that I would have allowed that to happen.

In that single day, that commander lost all possible respect from his men. Every one of them felt betrayed, myself included, and for the rest of his command, after I was reassigned, I would hear a number of horror stories about how terrible he was. Had that captain treated his soldiers the way he would treat his own loved ones, I'm sure he could have been much more successful.

I have tried to apply this principle to every workplace since, as an underlying and governing principle. As a leader your employees will notice, even when you don't.

I had taken over a team in the civilian world, and a couple months in, one of my employees surprised me in our one on one conversation. He was not a stellar performer and I had been preparing for a tough conversation. I came to the conversation with my usual line of questions:

1. What is going well?
2. What do I need to do better?
3. What do you like most about your job?
4. If you were in charge what would you change?

After I asked my first question, this technician responded, "I like how you treat everyone equally and don't tolerate disrespect." I smiled, "Oh? What do you mean?" "You know, like that time you didn't allow anyone to talk smack about that guy that wasn't there." I had literally no idea what this technician was talking about.

Apparently, we had a meeting with the entire team, and guys started ribbing each other like they often do. I tolerate it when it's in good fun, especially if it's a healthy competition (much like the two soldiers firing grenades in Afghanistan). This one day, however, someone made a comment about an employee that wasn't there, and it seemed to border the line between good fun and insulting. The technician recounted how I stopped it immediately and told them if they wouldn't say it to his face that I didn't want to hear it when he wasn't here.

This was a passing moment, one that I still don't even remember. At the time it wasn't a big deal to me at all, but for that technician in the crowd, it meant the world to him. He knew that I would stand up for *him*, even if he wasn't there, because I did it for someone else. That was a powerful message, not just for this particular technician, but for the team as a whole.

I later found out that the rest of the team had seen it as a pivotal moment and leadership shift that they had not seen before. There was a time when that behavior was condoned, and the leadership would even join in. My subordinate team leaders told me they knew things would be very different when that happened.

You never know what act, or which statement is going to be the one that allows someone to form a lasting opinion about you (good or bad). This is why it is important to always operate under a certain set of personal rules, and those rules are made easier to follow when they are governed by simple thoughts. If you remember that everyone is the most important person in the world to someone and treat them as though they were the most important person in the world to you, you will never fail and one day have your own highly influential moment that you don't remember either.

Take Action:

Next time someone confronts you with information regarding unacceptable behavior from someone in your team, respond with,

"Ok, thanks, I'll look into it." Then, when you talk to the employee say, "Tell me what happened with…" These statements don't assign culpability to anyone and will let you get both sides of a story. They keep people from putting their guard up, and they will keep you from putting your foot in your mouth.

14. Time for a tough conversation

Being a leader means that one day you are going to have to have a difficult conversation. You will maybe need to discipline someone, or worst case, fire them. If you bought into the principle outlined in the previous chapter, then you may have already wondered how to pursue discipline under those governing principles.

First off, disciplinary action needs to be your last action (except in matters dealing with safety or egregious violations). You should be having regular one on one conversations with your subordinates which are opportunities to provide the purpose, direction, and motivation your employees need to succeed. This should drastically reduce your need to pursue punitive discipline, but occasionally it happens. In the following section, the names of the employees have been changed for their protection.

"You need to talk to Jerry, he was way out of line with me yesterday." A fellow supervisor came and found me. One of my employees had entered his area and was cursing out his employees for some work they had done. When this supervisor confronted Jerry, Jerry was rude and disrespectful then walked away. My hand seemed forced, but over the years I have learned that every story has another side. Before rushing to judgement, I generally give myself a way out in case I'm wrong. I responded, "I've had to talk to him about his conversation style in the past. I'll make sure to talk to him today about this to find out what happened."

That afternoon, when Jerry came in, I asked him to join me in a private office for a brief conversation. We sat down, "You want to tell me what happened with Mike last night?" Jerry went on to describe the events. He was clearly still mad about the workmanship but having had a night to think about his actions, it was clear he knew he was out of line (even if he didn't expressly state it).

"Well Jerry, you know you were out of line. You also know that I will not tolerate that kind of behavior, but more importantly, YOU should not tolerate that kind of behavior. I know you care about the quality of your work and the way people perceive the work you do. You should also know that if you are rude and disrespectful, it doesn't matter how good your work is, you won't last long here. I want to discuss with you about an action plan on how you can fix this and how I can help you…"

While the actual conversation involved more back and forth, and it was certainly more verbose, the key highlights are noted above. What I really want to impress upon you is how to have these types of conversations. I'm sure you've heard in the past that the way to give bad news is to sandwich it between good news. These conversations go something like this:

You're awesome!
You suck!
You're awesome!

This is often known as the bad news sandwich. It's an ineffective, and terrible way to communicate. The person receiving this feedback often leaves confused, and even less often changes their behavior.

Another technique I've seen in disciplinary hearings is the "it's not that bad" approach. This often is a supplemental to the bad news sandwich. It looks like this:

You're awesome!
You suck!
It's ok, I've done it before too!
You're awesome!

If you are actually writing someone up and taking their pay and you take this approach, there's a 50/50 chance they will use it against you. More importantly, if your goal is to coach and mentor out the bad behavior, this approach is never going to achieve that desired result.

Over the years I have developed a different model for difficult conversations:
This is what you did (facts only)
This is unacceptable
Here is how it doesn't fit with your own principles
Let's make an action plan to fix it

124

If you look back at my conversation with Jerry, you can see how I took this approach in action. First, I confirmed that the actions were indeed true. Once Jerry had confirmed his accusations, then I needed to tell him it was unacceptable. Next, I pointed out how his behavior did not align with his very own principles and that he should be disappointed in himself. Finally, we made a plan together on how to fix it.

The next day his supervisor came to find me. "Louis, what the hell did you say to Jerry?" I looked at him shocked, "Um, I don't know, I told him his behavior was unacceptable. Why?" He looked at me through his thick white beard and smiled big enough to bear his teeth, "He's a completely new man! I can't believe it Louis! I've never seen anything like it!" He put his huge hand on my shoulder and leaned down, "You told that guy he was a piece of crap and he thanked you for it!" I smiled big, "Well, I didn't really tell him he was a piece of crap, but...ok, great news!"

Months later Jerry still hadn't resorted back to his old ways and I consistently got feedback from other employees who worked with him about how thorough he was and what a great job he was doing. I made sure to let Jerry know that his teammates had noticed a turnaround. It was a great victory for our team and our company.

Sometimes, however, the stories don't end on such a high note, and you have to make the extremely difficult decision to let someone go.

"Louis, you need to come outside right now." I could see the concern on the technician's face and immediately knew that something was gravely wrong. I grabbed my safety glasses and followed him outside. We turned a corner and I saw one of the machines nearly off the stands.

We were in the process of completely rebuilding a large Caterpillar loader for one of our clients. At this location we offered a service where a client could bring in a machine, have it torn down completely to the bare frame, and then have every component reconditioned or replaced to "like new" condition. It allowed them to get a machine with a warranty and the same use life as a new one for a fraction of the cost.

This particular build was in the later stages. The 60,000 pound machine still didn't have tires on it and was being rebuilt on stands about 4 feet off the ground. This technician decided to remove a safety lock on the machine and turn the wheel. This caused the entire front end to articulate and nearly come off the stand. Miraculously it didn't fall and kill him and people near him. Only a few inches of the machine were resting on one of the rear stands and another few inches on the center by the articulation. It took the team hours and multiple cranes to safely get the machine back on stands properly.

We spent a long time talking about safety with this technician, and frankly, I debated firing him just on this infraction alone. He was a young guy, however, with limited experience. He also had a great attitude, was always willing to do the terrible jobs, never complained, and was eager to learn. So, we gave him another chance.

Less than a month later I saw a safety observation come across my desk. Someone laid a 500 pound wheel hub on the curved edge of a table and walked away. The hub rolled off the table and slammed violently onto the shop floor. When I went to investigate, I learned that it was once again this same young technician.

At this point, continuing to let him work in my shop was putting him and other technicians around him at risk. As a leader, I have a responsibility to all my employees to keep them safe and send them home each day the same way they came in. I take that responsibility seriously and am unwilling to compromise when it comes to matters of safety. Despite regular coaching conversations, and the gravity of the issue he had already had, this technician simply seemed to struggle understanding common sense safety operating procedures. He was going to get someone hurt.

I spoke to my bosses and called our human resources department to let them know I was going to separate him. I filled out the necessary paperwork, sent it in and went home. I knew it would take at least a day to get everything back. I labored over my decision all night. I knew that this employee was a good guy who wanted to do well. He was highly motivated and was excited to work for our company. I also knew that he was in a protracted custody battle for his daughter, and this certainly wasn't going to help him.

I barely slept. The next day, when everything had been approved, I got the leadership team together and discussed how everything would go down. We made our plan and I called him in. I followed my same approach and explained the pattern of behavior that we had observed. Prior to starting with me, he had a couple safety incidents, then two more while working in my shop. I told him how his actions were putting himself and the technicians around him at risk. I had a responsibility to every member of my team to keep them safe, and because of that, I had to let him go.

He understood and was actually in about as good a spirit as one can be when getting this kind of news. He assured us that he would get better so when we hired him back in the future it would be an easy decision. I wished him luck, helped him pack his stuff, and signed him out.

That night I had a drink.

In almost 20 years of leadership, I've only had to do that a small handful of times. Overwhelmingly most of my "disciplinary" conversations are like the one I had with Jerry. Once you outline expectations, earn trust, and develop a game plan, most people will respond to that and start adjusting their behavior.

I supervised a union shop for a couple years, and frankly, it was the least successful years of leadership in my entire career. Many of my leadership tools were taken away, and the relationship between supervision and employee was highly structured and contractual. The opportunities to promote people are extremely limited since seniority is more important than individual performance. It was also my first position after I left the military and I struggled to adapt my leadership style to this new environment.

The first few months were particularly difficult. I received some less than stellar advice on how to lead my team, but thankfully I realized it quickly and went back to the tried and true methods that I have outlined in this book. The change was dramatic, enough so that my team recognized it and we finally began to click as a team.

I had one employee in particular who was a bit difficult to work with. His performance wasn't always ideal and being low on the seniority totem pole meant that he was regularly frustrated with his afforded opportunities. Using our one on ones, I learned more about him and what motivated him. Finally, one day we had a similar "disciplinary" discussion. From that discussion we came out with a plan.

Over the next few months, his performance dramatically improved. He became a key player in the team, taking on additional responsibilities, always willing to help others, and coming up with great ideas on how to improve our productivity. I was shocked the day he showed up at my desk and asked me if I would help him apply for college.

It was an exciting day when he was accepted, and we were able to celebrate together. Before I left he got a new position on the Continuous Improvement team for the factory and was well on his way to earning his degree.

When I look back at my tenure as a supervisor in a union environment, the greatest victories I had as a leader were not improving productivity or quality, but helping guys improve their positions from going to college, becoming leaders in the union, moving guys into highly skilled jobs, and one guy even got elected to the city council.

Without applying the discussion methodology outlined previously, none of that would have been possible. In addition, by showing a willingness to sit down and get feedback from my own employees about *my* performance, I learned what I needed to change. If I didn't have my particular approach to disciplinary conversations, the results would have likely been more punitive and not had such a positive impact overall.

Take Action:

Mark page 120 of this book and highlight how to conduct discipline. The next time you are facing this type of situation, use it as a reference and plan out your write-up and the ensuing conversation.

15. Delegate Responsibility, Not Authority

North Carolina, 2015

One of my positions with John Deere was as a Program Manager (PM) bringing new products to market. It's an interesting role that allowed me to manage the entire product lifecycle from technology development, building a business case, testing equipment, customer touch points, testing, building new assembly lines, starting production, and finally assessing the market acceptance. Deere is a large organization with a rigid product development process, multiple reporting requirements, and leadership decision gates where you have to meet certain metrics in order to receive funding or continue moving forward with the product.

I was hired on for one particular program, the one I talked about earlier in the book that had been on the shelf for years and I pressured executives to make a decision to allow us to move forward. Because I was a junior PM, I was only given a single program to manage and I did not have any direct reports.

In the Army, young officers that have shown a particular affinity for a command position are usually placed into an assistant planning and operations officer role. You work directly for the planning and operations officer, and often run meetings, build reports, and provide guidance. Similar to the PM role, you have to work with all areas of the organization, you have no direct reports, and you have to lead through influence not authority.

The previous program manager was also the lead design engineer and so was very involved with the details of the project attempting to do much of the work himself. He had also strained relationships with other areas of the organization like Supply Management, Marketing, Manufacturing, and even the leadership team. The morale of the team was extremely low, and the project was not expected to ever get off the ground.

Once I was handed the reigns, I started discussions with each member of the team, getting their unique perspectives, and assessing what was going well and what we needed to improve as a team. I realized that many of them saw this as a side project, and most of the work was done for them, so individual ownership was lacking. Team meetings were usually a one-way conversation where the PM would hand out tasks, dominate the conversation, then close out the meeting. Presentations to leadership were also almost universally handled by the PM. Essentially, there was little to no delegation going on.

I started giving more individual ownership to each member of the team. I expected team members to present their portion of the discussion not only at the team meetings, but at leadership briefings as well. Our meetings also changed from informational updates to task and action item list. Finally, I instituted a round table before the

132

meeting was adjourned where I individually asked every member of the team if they had any final questions, comments, or concerns.

This sent a clear message: Everyone had an important opinion, and we were in this project together. It didn't take long for the team to embrace the changes.

From my one on one conversations with the executive leadership team (yes, I conduct them with superiors as well), I also was able to determine what some of the sources of apprehension were at higher levels and brought those to the team. The creativity of all these great people was unleashed, which was our greatest strength. Together, with each person involved, we were able to develop several courses of action, with fully developed business plans and schedules that had pros and cons which addressed each executive's concerns. This due diligence, made possible through the power of delegation, was the key in getting the project approved and moving forward for the first time in years.

Not long after the project was approved and moving forward, I noticed my supervisor was stressing out because a different PM had gotten another job and she had no one to take on his project. It was a relatively simple project. One of our partner companies was becoming a competitor and was no longer going to build a piece of equipment for us. The project goal was to bring the assembly into our factory and continue selling product. Very little testing should have been required, and the factory master plan already had a layout for the assembly line.

I volunteered to take on the project. My supervisor looked at me skeptically. "That's a senior program manager, and you want to take it on as an additional duty?" I smiled with conviction, "I'm certain I can handle it." She smiled back, paused for a moment, then answered, "ok."

In one three-minute conversation I had more than doubled my workload. The PM in charge of this project was working solid 12 hour days, I was pushing 10 daily. I now had to figure out how to cram a 22 hour day into 10 hours (I really wasn't interested in spending more time than that in the office). I had an ace up my sleeve, however. I knew that in typical fashion, that program manager had taken on the lion's share of the workload of his team.

Delegation is a lost art. I don't know you, but I guarantee you can finish this sentence: "If you want something done right…"

Exactly, it's a stupid saying and really reflects more on the individual saying it than on the person or people they are talking about. Proper delegation means that you have clearly outlined the purpose, the expectation, and are available to help accomplish the task. It also means being willing to accept the job done a little differently than you would do it.

I took the same approach to the new team as I had with the first. Meetings and tasks took on a collaborative approach. Not only did this release the creativity of the team, but it also made them more willing to speak up about issues and problems that had previously been pushed under the rug. The previous PM was not interested in hearing about problems and had chosen to ignore them outright, set unrealistic expectations, then cemented failure by briefing the leadership team that they were on track. Within a month of assuming the project I uncovered a host of issues from performance problems, manufacturing faults, quality misses, budget overruns and more.

I knew that we needed to get this information in front of the executive team immediately, but if we simply presented a slew of issues without resolution, it would paint this hard-working team in a terrible light. I sat down with each team member individually. We discussed the issues they were seeing, and together developed a course of action to correct it. I also asked each of them to prepare to brief our executive leaders on the plan of action.

These team members had never been given the authority to make decisions and come up with solutions. Solutions were dictated to them, and any issues they had were either completely ignored or silenced by decree. One person told me, "It feels like shackles have been taken off me and I can finally do my job!"

What we faced was a Mount Everest of challenges, and after some deliberation and teamwork, we came up with a follow-on program that would solve our cost overruns and allow us to update the design of the machine to meet our stringent quality and manufacturing standards. That meant that we would go to market with the current project, but immediately had to start on another to address the issues we had found.

My workload now increased from two programs to three.

I split up my team to run concurrent projects and added a few members. Some people would have to take on double duty, but everyone was ready to take on the challenge. Since they had been given the authority to make decisions, knowing that the responsibility of failure rested with me, team members came up with more audacious solutions to monumental challenges. Although it was a painful process, with a tremendous effort, we were able to launch our product within a few months of the original planned date. The second project was well underway, and it too launched as scheduled. It involved a major change to the factory and a creation of another entire assembly line.

Within a year of taking the PM job, I had successfully taken on three different programs. Soon I was asked to take on three more, and using the same successful model of delegation of authority, my responsibility ballooned to more than $20 million in R&D and was giving work direction to over 90 employees in multiple factories on multiple continents. I had a program for every single commercial mowing product in the John Deere offering, and I managed to do it in a 10 hour day...a busy one, but 10 hours nonetheless.

I want you to understand how to properly delegate tasks, because if you do it wrong it can destroy team morale and make you look lazy. Delegation is NOT simply passing off your work to someone else. You also don't get to delegate responsibility for the task. If you delegate a task, and the individual fails, it's your fault, and you must bear the burden of answering why that task was not completed appropriately. This is vital to understand, and although I've already said it more than once, it bears repeating yet again:

You can delegate authority but not responsibility!

When you delegate something, you need to make sure you ask yourself if it's a task you can even delegate first. For instance, an employee review or a disciplinary action are not tasks that you can delegate. You must do those yourself. Then you need to figure out who you can delegate the task to. This requires that you really know your people before you do it. Here are some questions to ask yourself before delegating a task:

1. Does this person have time to do this task?
2. Does it fit within their career goals?
3. Are they capable of completing the task?
4. Do they want to do it?

Let me explain each question a little more in depth.

1. Does this person have time to do this task?

This is a pretty obvious question. You don't want to overload someone who is already struggling to keep up with their current duties...with some exceptions. It may be that the individual you are thinking of delegating a task to is not very good at time management. They fill their day with superfluous, unnecessary tasks with the appearance of being busy while accomplishing little. In this case, it could be appropriate to give them an additional duty that would put pressure on finding a way to manage their time better.

Another way employees may be inappropriately filling their schedule is with additional breaks or they are long winded in their conversations. Giving them an additional task could help stop some of those breaks from happening. You may also have someone who isn't particularly skilled at something, so it takes them longer to complete the task. People that haven't been trained on certain software programs will be a lot slower with those programs (I'm thinking things like MS Office or simply being unable to type), so tasks that shouldn't take long take them longer. In this case, helping them work through an additional task would give you an opportunity to train them and give them an additional skill they didn't previously have.

For these reasons, you need to put some thought into deciding whether someone has enough time or not. Most people will stay "busy" all day while they are in the office. This doesn't automatically mean that they cannot accomplish the task.

2. Does this fit with their career goals?

Matching tasks to career goals is an exceptionally powerful tool of delegation. If your employees see that they are being given tasks that will allow them to be more competitive for future positions that they desire, they will be very excited to take them on and they will do them extraordinarily well.

In project Lightning, one of the junior engineers had expressed an interest to me in either being an engineering lead or a future program manager. His name was Taylor, and he was an outstanding design engineer. His peers looked up to him, and regularly asked him questions or asked him to look over their work. He was a natural leader, and I knew that giving him more opportunities for leadership would not only be more beneficial for his career, but also for our company as a whole.

Taylor's boss was the acting lead engineer on the project. I sat down with him and explained what I had observed in Taylor. I also discussed the future goals that Taylor had, and asked if he would be willing to allow Taylor to take on the lead engineer role for our project. We discussed the plan in depth, and while there was some hesitation at first, eventually Taylor's repeated outstanding performance was the deciding factor in his boss agreeing to the plan. Taylor was excited to take on the role, and he did an amazing job.

3.   Are they capable of completing the task?

This is another question that at first glance may seem like an obvious question with an easy answer, but you have to remember you're dealing with people, not robots. Sometimes our expectations of a person's capabilities are not met, and we have to adjust course.

As a leader, I'm always looking for people for future leadership positions. Typically, I like to give people who are showing potential a small leadership role to see how they handle it. It's like an extended interview, and later when I make a recommendation for a role, there is a ton of data I can fall back on to support my suggestion.

In one particular organization, I picked a guy who I will call Barry. He seemed like a great fit at first. The men valued his opinion, and he was capable of moving people to action. His attitude at times could suffer, but I had a feeling that with proper guidance and leadership, I could turn him around and use his influence to benefit the company.

At first, things were going really well. Barry stepped up big time. He was mentoring peers, taking initiative, and he brought great insight and value to our leadership discussions. As the weeks went on, however, I noticed his workmanship was taking a slip. He completed a large project and it was significantly over budget, late, and had quality issues after it was delivered to our client. Barry and I had a discussion and made a plan for the future.

He was in the middle of his second project when he asked if we could sit and talk in private. Barry was having significant marital problems. Through tears in his eyes, he told me that he needed to step down from the leadership role because he was so distracted at work. It took a lot of courage for him to be so open and honest with me. It also took incredible courage for him to recognize that he was not meeting the expectations of a future leader in our organization and ask to step down from the role.

I have tremendous respect for people who are willing to admit when they have made a mistake, because it is not easy to do. Even more so when your admission is going to have an adverse effect on your career. We talked for a long time, and while I had respect and empathy for his plight, I also had a responsibility to the team and I could not allow him to continue in the role. I agreed that he needed to step down but made sure to tell him that it was a very mature and courageous act to talk to me about this problem. Since he asked, I gave him my thoughts on his personal issue, with some insights on how he could work on his problems. I also let him know, once he had his life figured out, we could talk again about a leadership role.

Sometimes the unexpected is going to happen. Sometimes you might have every indicator that a person can do a job until you put them in it. You have to be willing to admit you need to make a change and take action.

4. Do they want to do it?

If someone doesn't want to do a task, they may not do it well. This does not necessarily mean that you shouldn't delegate the task anyway, but generally it's preferable to make sure the individual receiving the task is interested in doing it.

One notable exception was when I was delegating presentation responsibilities to each functional area as a program manager. One employee, I'll call her Maria, really didn't want to make or present her slides. Previously she would send raw data in an email, then the program manager would make the slide, present it, and Maria would be present in the room if there were any questions he could not answer. I was turning this methodology on its head. I would give each functional area an expectation of what needed to be presented, then they would make the slide, present it, and I would be in the room and available to help them answer any particularly difficult questions from the executive team.

Maria had a strong accent in English, and she wasn't particularly fast on PowerPoint. She was not looking forward to taking on this task and was consistently exploring ways to get out of it. I sat down with her and helped her build a format for her information. I also offered to review everything with her from her slide content to her actual presentation. I also made sure to discuss this with her supervisor and asked him to provide additional support in content creation and presentation.

At first, this was a lot of time and effort, but I knew I was making an investment that would pay dividends in the future. We had to give monthly updates, and each month she got better. She became more confident in her presentation, and needed less help preparing her slides. After a few months, she didn't need my help in slide creation nor in preparing her presentation. We also experienced the added bonus in her becoming a more active player in the team meetings as well. It became clear that while she struggled to communicate, both in delivery and clarity, she was extremely knowledgeable in her job and functional area.

Commander's Intent and End state

So you have identified the right person for the job and answered the necessary questions, and you are ready to delegate an appropriate task. The process for actually delegating a task is more involved than just, "I need you to do this."

Properly delegating a task requires the leader to clearly set expectations on what the task is, what it should accomplish, and why it must be done. In the military, with every operation order, is a section titled "Commander's Intent and End state". Ask any military commander and they will tell you that with a proper intent and end state, they can accomplish any mission.

The intent describes the commander's overarching rules on how the mission should be accomplished, the purpose, and how success will be defined. It's a method for setting boundaries while giving maximum freedom to subordinate commanders. We can never predict what the enemy will do or how they will react, and execution rarely, if ever, goes exactly according to plan. Subordinate leaders need to have the freedom to operate, call audibles, and make changes. As long as they understand the intent and end state, mission success can still be achieved.

Delegating a task is the same as giving an intent and end state. You must tell the person what the task is, what the purpose of the task is, what it should accomplish, and what the end result should be. You must also strike a careful balance between being specific enough that the purpose of the task can be accomplished, but broad enough that people can be creative in how they accomplish the task. I've spent some time thinking about some general rules that I could give you to execute this, but honestly there isn't some magical catch-all formula. The best I can tell you is to ask yourself if a particular part of the task is actually required or if it's just your personal preference. If it's your personal preference, then don't make it a requirement.

My teams were high performing, and the returns on our projects averaged over 20%. One project more than doubled in ROI from project approval to launch. We changed the layout of the factory and brought in thousands more units of production. We also improved the performance of our machines and delivered new technologies through partnerships that had never been released to the market before.

All of this was accomplished because I empowered individuals to make decisions and have ownership over their portion of the project. I learned something very valuable in that experience: If you want something done right…unleash the creative power of your team!

Take Action:

Find one thing to delegate this week. Use the methodology outlined in this chapter to identify the right person, then make sure you give them the tools necessary to be successful.

16. Beware of Toxic leaders

There are good leaders, bad leaders, and toxic leaders. Good leaders are the people that execute all or most of the principles outlined in this book, they are humble, confident, have a servant mentality, and care for their people. In addition, they help mentor and motivate their employees, and they deliver results. Bad leaders can have the same humility and servant attitude, sometimes even care for their people, but they don't know how to provide purpose, direction and motivation to their employees. They also don't know how to mentor and guide their employees to improve their careers. A toxic leader is different, and much more dangerous to your organization.

Toxic leaders rarely know they are toxic. They often are capable of delivering results (at least for a short time). Toxic leaders know the right terminology and are very good at keeping their bosses happy. I've also noticed that many of them were excellent individual performers. What makes toxic leaders anathema to an organization is their attitude and approach to their subordinates.

I have worked for toxic leaders in the past. One of them was the guy who called the wrong call sign and made everyone think they were deploying. These people exist in virtually every organization. They rise to leadership ranks because they are smart and capable, but they will destroy your organization because they lack empathy, they do not care for anyone but themselves, and they are totally indifferent to the career goals and aspirations of their subordinates. Sometimes a toxic leader will even actively prohibit or obstruct their employees from getting positions of higher pay and responsibility because they want to keep their team intact.

Toxic leaders rule with fear. They love writing people up and thrive on conflict. Their conversations are usually one-sided, and they are quick to smash any opposition to their ideas. Toxic leaders have no problem criticizing peers and subordinates, both in private and in public. They will also criticize their supervisors, but only in private as they attempt to build coalitions. They are disloyal to anyone who is not in a position to benefit them personally.

Toxic leaders are smart and cunning. They are deliberate in their decisions, and because they are always looking out for their own best interests, sometimes those interests align with the company goals. This is part of the reason why so many of them continue to get promoted in organizations, leaving a trail of despair behind them.

Like I mentioned, most toxic leaders don't even realize they are one. Here are some simple questions to help you identify if you are actually a toxic leader:

1. What is more valuable to you, a "good job" from your boss or your subordinates?
2. When a problem occurs, do you think first how to fix it or who to blame?
3. When you look back at your career, what are you most proud of? Personal success or your subordinate's success?
4. Do you believe fear is a powerful motivator?
5. Do you take the time to know the people that work for you? Do you know their families? Their goals? Their hobbies?

If praise from your boss means more to you, if you always look to assign blame, if your personal success is most important, if you believe fear is a powerful motivator, and you don't know your subordinates, then you are a toxic leader.

All of the behaviors of a toxic leader stem from the foundational principle on which they operate: arrogance. The toxic leaders have had some success in the past, and they genuinely believe they have all the answers. This is what makes them particularly dangerous to an organization. They look down on their subordinates, even more so if they once did the job. No one can ever do the job as good as they did (in their mind). They are persistent complainers, but shroud their complaints in criticisms of performance by those around them. They are also careful to complain only to the coalitions they have built.

There are some of you that are good leaders, but have subordinate leaders that are toxic and don't even know it (Let me just say, if you know that a subordinate is a terrible leader and you leave him or her in that position, you are just as at fault for the stress, pain, and cost that the toxic leader causes, and you are a coward). So I'm going to give you some tips in order to identify these people.

You are looking for someone that places the organization above their subordinates. For instance, think back at that commander who called us all in thinking we were going to deploy. He genuinely didn't care at all that guys were hugging their crying kids in the parking lot. His concern was that his unit was ready to deploy in less than two hours, and that's probably what he told the battalion commander.

You are looking for someone that has no trouble accepting praise and rarely gives anyone else credit. Find someone who is a leader of a team and praise them individually for things the team has accomplished. If they don't correct you and tell you that it was a group effort, it's time to do some more investigation, because you might have a toxic leader in front of you. It's also possible that you have a serious introvert who is nervous about the conversation, so don't jump to a conclusion without further investigation.

Ask them what they think of their peers, if they have mostly negative things to say, then you likely have a toxic leader. Good leaders are team players. Their first impulse is to give praise. If they are going to give you negative feedback about someone (because sometimes it's warranted), they will usually tell you what that individual's strengths are and where they could be placed to maximize those strengths. A toxic leader is not concerned with helping people improve and are more than happy to convince you to drop someone who they think is a non-performer.

When something goes wrong, see if they tell you who was at fault instead of how to fix the problem. The first impulse of a toxic leader is to place blame and pursue discipline. Remember that they lead through fear. Every problem in the organization, in the eyes of a toxic leader, boils down to individuals or other organizations that do not perform well. In fact, the first fact finding mission for the toxic leader is who to blame. Rather than identify opportunities for organizational and process improvement, the toxic leader is only looking to place blame. A good leader is going to take the blame for problems. They will never point fingers, instead their fact-finding missions will be centered on finding root causes and process solutions to eliminate the possibility of the problem occurring again in the future.

Talk to their subordinates. How often do you sit down with people two levels down or more from you? I keep stressing the importance of one on one conversations with your direct reports, but just as important is to have those conversations with people all through your organization. I don't care how large your organization is, if you make it a priority, you can find time to talk to someone at every level of your organization; and you should.

I'm talking to the senior executive reading this right now who is already dismissing this possibility because you have thousands of employees. If the sergeant major of the army, an organization with over 500,000 employees, can find time to talk to privates and junior leaders wherever he goes, so can you. When you visit locations outside of your headquarters, do you sit down with the employees or the senior leaders in charge? You and I both know how these visits actually go...

Someone on your staff alerts a team that you are on your way. The folks at that location spend days getting ready for your visit. When you arrive, everything is in pristine condition, they have a very well organized tour, and a series of well-rehearsed presentations. You may have a lunch with a select few individuals, but even they are hand-picked, and rarely does the conversation move past the

148

superficial level. If you really want to get a feel for the health of your organization, you need to first lead by example and start doing one on ones with your subordinates one and two levels down. When you go to a location, you need to have a small group discussion 2-5 people who are all at the same level, without their supervisors present. This will send a clear message that will permeate throughout your organization, and soon everyone will be doing the same thing.

I can't stress enough how important it is to find those toxic leaders and either coach out the behavior, or root them out. Someone who doesn't care about employees who is in a leadership position is like a nuclear bomb to morale. These people negatively influence not only their own teams, but adjacent units as well. Their mere presence reduces productivity and drives away your best leaders. Your team cannot thrive with toxic leaders in the midst.

Take Action:

This one is for leaders of leaders only. Your subordinate leaders are a direct reflection of you. How do you want to be represented? It is your responsibility to go out and find those toxic leaders and get rid of them. You should have already scheduled those one on ones, now make sure you are asking the questions I told you to ask in this chapter. Now you can set one on ones with people two levels below and see if your subordinate leaders are being great stewards of your organization.

17. Awards and Recognition

Afghanistan, 2006

"I don't want it." Captain Teague had just told me that I would be getting a Bronze Star for my service during the deployment. The award was being given out by rank, as a blanket award. To me, this cheapened the medal considerably, and some of the people getting the award were certainly not deserving of it. I was particularly upset because the medals had become more of a political game than rewards based on merit.

I had put in one of my squad leaders who was a fierce warrior, for a second Bronze Star with Valor in the same deployment. It was denied because, "he already has one." I was furious and raised quite a stink about it. Eventually I lost the fight with the bureaucracy, but being a young combat officer, it bred a level of resentment in me that was difficult to let go. When I heard about the blanket awards based on rank, I staged my own personal coup in protest.

Captain Teague pulled me into his hooch to have a conversation about it. I unloaded with all the unfairness I had seen and explained my frustrations. In his typical fashion, Teague allowed me to talk, then took a moment to think before responding. "Louis, you can keep with this attitude, or you can act like a leader. This award is not for you, it's for them," he pointed in the general direction of my platoon bays. I looked at him quizzically and he continued, "for the rest of your life, you will have that medal. When people ask you what you did to earn it, you will get to tell them the stories about the amazing men of 3rd platoon that you had an opportunity to lead."

His words hit me like a Mack truck. I hadn't taken the time to consider this perspective. While I still wasn't happy with the way some of the medals for my platoon had been handled, I had to concede that Teague was right. The best way to honor those men and what they had done, was to wear the medal and always give them the credit for it. It afforded me the opportunity to remember the legacy and valor of great men and how blessed I was to have gotten to know them.

Because of my personal experience, I resolved to always recognize my employees for jobs well done. Even if I couldn't award them with something, I could certainly let them know how I felt. A sincere thank you, with a specific description of what an employee has done to go above and beyond is a powerful motivational tool.

While the military has a standard for awards and recognition, in the civilian world this is lacking. In the same way that leaders are taught that they need to improve weaknesses, they are also taught that they need to constantly give instruction and counsel on how to improve. The problem with this approach is that when you constantly give negative advice, people start to believe your negativity.

I was observing a team that worked for a leader who was notorious for being unable to give positive feedback. I sat in the back of a large meeting room as the leader talked about the stretch goals he wanted the team to achieve. He clearly wasn't a perceptive speaker because the body language of the team was quite negative. There were shaking heads, arms crossed, and overall a sense of disbelief that they could achieve these new goals and standards that were being set.

When the meeting adjourned, I walked out with the group and overheard the comments of the team as they exited the room:

"There's no way dude."
"Why should we even try, we're going to get yelled at anyway"
"He's just setting us up to fail again."
"We can't even make our current goals and he wants to make them harder?"

They had already failed in their minds, and they hadn't even tried, but they were simply responding to all the months and years of negative reinforcement they had received on the part of this leader.

As the weeks went on, I saw what was going on. This leader seemed incapable of telling the team that they were doing a good job, even when it was merited. Whenever they met a goal, his response was typically "good job, but…" This incessant negativity began to take root in the minds of the team. They believed that they were not good enough and would always fall short. That's why, when they were given a difficult challenge, they already decided that they weren't good enough to make it.

If you want to lead and influence people to unleash their creative abilities, you're not going to do it by constantly giving negative feedback. Eventually people stop listening to you and they give up trying to do better. Your voice becomes the Charlie Brown teacher: background noise.

I doubt that your goal as a leader is to become background noise, an uninspiring voice that is ignored at best and resented at worst. You can't drive people and teams to improve and change if you have lost your ability to influence.

This is probably the most common fault I see among leaders all over the world. I had a subordinate leader in my organization once who had built a very strong and cohesive team. I saw how his team interacted with each other and how much they would go out of their way to help each other. They operated like a family, often going to lunch together, giving each other advice on how to handle problems, and always motivating each other. What I found was that their leader made it a point to go out of his way to congratulate team members whenever they did a great job. He would also send messages to senior leaders when team members went above and beyond. Because of his motivational style, that team had grown closer together and took on challenges with excitement.

Because he had shown that he cared, and believed in them and what they could accomplish, they had become a top performing team that enjoyed taking on stretch goals. They believed in themselves and genuinely felt like they could accomplish any task. They were a team of winners, made so through positive reinforcement and encouragement.

This doesn't mean that you can just go around telling people "good job" and that somehow is going to motivate them. If your praise doesn't focus on a specific act or behavior, it's going to appear disingenuous and unbelievable. Rather than simply saying, "hey, you're doing a great job," try something like, "Hey, I really appreciated when you went out of your way to help your teammate. This is exactly what I would like to see more of and you are setting an example of the type of leadership our team needs!" The second example is a specific task and why that task was something that will really improve the team. It's honest and unambiguous.

With the proper motivational attitude, you can drive your team to continue doing the types of actions that will improve the organization. The people on your team need to hear what they are doing well so they continue to do it, and even do more of it!

Take Action:

This week you need to go out and give someone praise. Not just "good job" but identify a specific thing that person has done that was really exemplary. Tell them what it was, why it was awesome, and how it helps the team. Then make sure you do it every single week from now on. Soon it will become a habit and you won't even need to purposefully think about it before you find yourself doing it.

Keep On Leading People: A summary

G reat leaders win by influencing and moving people to action. This can only be achieved when you start with a servant leader attitude. When you realize that you exist to serve your team and take the time to value them as individuals, then you can start to influence the team as a whole.

Get to know the people on your team. Find out what gets them excited, how they are best motivated, and what they look forward to about their work. Understand what challenges they face, what makes their job difficult, and what their sources of frustration are, then work to eliminate those problems.

Learn what each person on your team is good at, then develop those strengths. Put people in positions where they can do what they love best, and they will deliver for you. Stop focusing on weaknesses! Train and develop people on their strengths. They will be happier and will do much better work.

Remember that everyone on your team is the most important person in the world to somebody. They are not numbers or tools, they are people with specific needs and wants, and they are all valuable! Treat them all with the utmost respect and fairness. Engage them and their ideas. Listen to what they have to say, especially when it's about your own conduct. Make time for everyone, follow up on their requests, and never put someone down or allow others to do so.

Remember the process for having difficult conversations. Don't sandwich bad news, but focus solely on the facts, the unacceptable behavior, and make a plan of action on how to fix that behavior *together*. Follow up and track the progress, making sure to acknowledge when the person is doing a great job.

Use delegation as a tool to develop your team and future leaders. Never say, "if you want something done right, you have to do it yourself." It degrades your team and makes them think that you don't trust them to do a good job. Give clear guidance, and remember that when you delegate, you still retain the responsibility for the task. Give people a chance to be creative.

Pay attention to toxic leaders. Don't allow them to flourish or even exist in your organization. Remember that you are looking for people who don't value the individuals on their team or their peers. They are quick to criticize and have no loyalty to anyone but themselves. They may be solid individual contributors, but they will destroy your organization from the inside if they are allowed to continue with their toxic behaviors.

Finally, make sure you take the time to give positive reinforcement. Motivate your employees and build their egos when they do a great job. Take the time to give specific examples of all the great things they are doing.

If you put forth the effort to lead individuals, you will be setting yourself up to move the group to massive action. When your team members know they can trust you to put their interests first, they will move mountains for you!

KEEP ON LEADING TEAMS

Introduction

Moving your team to action is the ultimate goal of every leader, from the CEO on down to the small team leader. When we evaluate leaders we do so based on overall team performance. That being said, moving a team to action is prohibitively difficult when you have not started by leading yourself and also the individuals in your team.

If you look at the major players and leading companies today, they all started from humble beginnings and a dream. The CEO's led themselves, pushed themselves, and made sacrifices in pursuit of their goals. As they grew, they brought more people in, sold them on the idea, led the people, and continued to lead their team. Eventually they became common household names: Henry Ford, Walt Disney, Bill Gates, Steve Jobs, Jeff Bezos, Gary Vaynerchuck, the list goes on, but the methodology and recipe for success is strikingly similar. Each of these leaders has a unique personality and style. Some are outgoing, some are introverts. Some have large personalities and love to share, others are more reserved, but all of them have successfully lead their teams to great success.

You might not be on the cusp of some major market disruption, but the principles of leadership still are just as important to improve productivity, eventually increase the bottom line, and drive your team to accomplish scary goals. Once you have successfully led yourself, and are in the process of leading your team, then you are ready to start setting some previously unachievable goals with the group.

I will show you how to set those scary goals and drive your team to achieve them. How to get buy-in from the team. How to influence your junior leaders to drive for results. We will discuss methods for improving morale, having fun, and recognizing the team. What kind of people you want to surround yourself with, and how to encourage the flow of ideas. We will also discuss how to stay calm in the face of adversity and why it's important.

While I haven't developed a company that changed the world, my teams have always out-performed our expectations, from not losing a single soldier in Afghanistan, to completely denying the enemy the ability to operate in our AO in Iraq, to bringing out new products in record time and ROI while at John Deere. I have never been ok with continuing the same behaviors, and my teams have always been eager to rise to the challenge and disrupt the status quo.

18. Stay Calm

Afghanistan, 2005

We had been walking for hours along the Afghan ridgelines heading towards Pakistan. After the massive attack on our base the night before, we gathered our forces and set out in pursuit of the enemy. The mountains were strewn with blood trails and hundreds of footprints. We were able to identify where the enemy had staged their attack, where their heavy weapons were set, and most shocking, where they had a casualty evacuation site.

We spotted an area on the backside of a nearby hilltop where it was clear there were dozens of trucks parked and a triage area where casualties had been evacuated across the border. The predator drone had spotted a group of men in a draw several miles away and fired a hellfire missile into their formation causing an undetermined number of casualties. That area was our eventual mission location, but in order to get there, we had to traverse miles of unforgiving terrain with potential pockets of enemy defenders along the way.

We stepped off not long after sunrise, most of us with just minutes of sleep under our belts before the attack had begun the previous night. By the time our mission started, the adrenaline had worn off, but we were sure to keep our minds alert to any potential threats; the enemy could literally be anywhere.

We patrolled the mountains for hours, on several occasions coming across abandoned homes, or terrain that would make for excellent ambush areas. We treated each one as though we were about to face the incoming hoard. Finally, late into the afternoon, we arrived at our confirmed enemy location.

My company commander was with me, and he split our unit in several forces. One would stay at the entrance of the draw to ensure we weren't outflanked. Another would clear along the ridge, taking the high ground, and a third would enter the draw and clear across the enemy location.

I took the team up the ridgeline up to around 8,000 feet of elevation. My men were used to the high elevations since I made it a habit of clearing the high ground any time we approached bottlenecks in the terrain. In 2005 most of the IED's we encountered were command detonated. This meant that there was usually someone nearby with a detonator of some sort and would manually set off the bomb as our units drove by. Because we took the extra time and effort to climb every mountain that presented an ideal location and opportunity for an ambush, and had done so for months, we did not get hit by a single IED that entire deployment. My men also were incredibly fit, agile, and comfortable at elevations. Despite our heavy gear, we were able to move as fast as the enemy in that same terrain. This took away our enemy's greatest advantage and was a key element in winning battles even though we were frequently outnumbered and in unfamiliar terrain.

We crested the ridgeline quickly and were clearing faster than the unit in the draw. Our movement was severely restricted, however, and we were forced to move single file through most of the area. My squad leader was in front, and I followed right behind him. After having learned some lessons early in the deployment, I started carrying the heavy radio pack myself which afforded us redundant communication and made my ability to call in support much easier. Due to our distance from the base, I had the long 10ft antenna up and extended completely.

My squad leader threw up his left hand in a "halt" hand signal. We stopped as he brought his weapon up and looked through his scope. "I have one enemy, alive. He has his weapon," he paused for a moment then with tension in his voice asked, "I think I'm spotted, can I shoot?" "Take the shot," I responded.

Bang, bang, bang, bang, bang, bang...he fired numerous rounds at the enemy. This squad leader was an excellent marksman and it was uncharacteristic for him to need more than one or two shots, let alone six. "I think he's dead," I interrupted. Not one second after I uttered my sentence did the enemy return fire. A burst of rounds accurately targeted our position. The rounds cracked off the rocks against my shoulder and a large branch that came out of the rocks shattered into a million pieces. We both jerked back and ducked. My squad leader let out a yelp and fell behind me. I raised my weapon and fired several rounds into the enemy's position. This seemed to quell the onslaught briefly and I looked back at my squad leader.

I thought at first that he had been hit, but when I turned around and saw him clutching his shoulder, I realized he hadn't been shot, but instead dislocated his shoulder when he jerked out of the way. I watched in awe as he slid his arm back into socket, then after uttering a slew of profanity, grabbed a rocket off his back. "Look out," he said the statement as a matter of fact. By the look on his face, I could tell there was no talking him out of firing his rocket, but there was no room to move, and I was in the path. I looked down at my feet and raised my leg to give him enough room to fire. The rocket launched, sending a wave of fire and heat across my leg, and slammed into a large rock formation in front of the enemy with a loud explosion.

Meanwhile, the volume of fire began to pick up again. The enemy was firing simultaneously down the draw and up into the ridgeline where we were. Less than a minute had gone by, and as I reached for my radio hand mic, I heard the call from the men in the draw. "BRAVO SIX IS IN CONTACT! BRAVO SIX IS IN CONTACT! ENEMY FIRE ON OUR POSITION..." One of the radio operators was yelling into the radio net, frantically letting our headquarters know that we were in a firefight. Because he was inside the draw, his communications were not being heard clearly, and in addition the screams were getting everyone on edge.

The information that we needed to convey to get our support network up and running was not getting out. In addition, our ability to communicate internally about enemy positions and friendly movement was being hindered by his shrieking communications. Finally, during a break in his transmissions, I jumped on the radio. By now, I had been in dozens of firefights and had learned the key to controlling the battle was staying calm. This allowed me to keep a clear head and understand the battle. It also instilled confidence in our supporting units that the information they were getting was accurate. Finally, it emboldened my own soldiers as they knew we had a plan and were moving to victory. I told him to stay off the radio, informed him and others that I was in the best position to see the entire battlefield, and due to my elevation, I had the clearest communication with our headquarters element.

The battle immediately seemed to slow down. Reports started going back and forth between the different units on what each of us was seeing. I was able to get air support on the way, and our attack became coordinated. We pushed forward from the ridgeline as the men in the draw were getting pinned down. We charged down the hill in a synchronized bounding maneuver covering each other's movements with a heavy volume of fire. By the time we got to the bottom, the remaining enemy forces were dead.

Your people will mimic your level of energy as a leader. I'm sure many of you have seen it before, the boss gets yelled at, then his subordinates get yelled at, then they yell at the people below them, and on it goes to the bottom. This kind of energy is not fruitful and it doesn't bring the best out of our teams. It creates strife, friction, and unhealthy competition. It quells creativity, and actually has an adverse effect on productivity as well. People move fast, but they get nowhere.

When leaders are angry, the teams assume that punitive actions will follow. Team members will be at each other's throats, and when problems occur, blame becomes a game of hot potato and finger pointing instead of collaborative solution finding. Your team can never achieve greatness and meet difficult goals if fear and stress rules the workplace. I knew that in order to keep my men safe, I needed to keep control of the battle. They had to know that I was in control in order to clearly follow orders and be able to let me know what they were seeing and observing. Anger and fear breed chaos, and chaos will destroy your team.

Some of you might be thinking, "I only get angry when things are bad and I want my people to know I'm serious." It sounds like a reasonable response but lashing out isn't going to get rid of whatever serious problem you are looking to fix. Instead it diminishes your impact with the team. I recommend in the place of anger, that you stay calm, assertive, and firm. If you are properly leading yourself and your people, letting the team know you are disappointed in a result or a particular action they have taken will have a much deeper and lasting impact than yelling.

I took over a team once in the civilian world that had team update meetings every Monday. The entire group would be there, they would discuss some safety topics and also general issues that needed to be addressed. When I took over, the meeting had been re-labeled the "Monday beatdown meeting." I watched during my transition period as the employees checked out as soon as they came in to the meeting room. Rarely, if ever, did any solutions come about in that meeting. Instead, creativity was squashed, and the employees did only enough to avoid getting yelled at. The angry leader creates a toxic environment, and as I have already discussed in depth, toxic environments will not bring the best out of your teams.

Next time you want to get angry to get your point across, take a moment and calm yourself down. Think about the reasons why this particular problem is such a big deal. Maybe it's a safety issue, maybe is a productivity issue, whatever the reason is, prepare to outline that clearly to the team. When you are in front of your team, clearly explain the problem and the ramifications of not fixing it.

Since you take this as a personal issue, they too will take it as a personal issue. Tell them something like, "I'm disappointed with the performance of this team. You usually don't have this problem, and if we are going to be the best, we need to fix this immediately." If you remember the format for disciplinary discussions, you can apply this same format to your discussion with the team:

This is what you did (facts only)

This is unacceptable

Here is how it doesn't fit with your own principles

Let's make an action plan to fix it

Sometimes you don't have time to have this kind of discussion with the group. For instance, in the firefight example at the beginning of this chapter, I certainly didn't have time for that type of a discussion. Instead I took control of the situation, remained calm, and gave orders in an assertive manner. The gravity of the situation was not missed on the squad, and they sprang into action...in a controlled manner.

Someone who is slamming the desk, throwing things, and yelling does not inspire anyone to action. Look at the team at the receiving end of one of those tirades and tell me if their faces scream creativity. Instead they have shut down, and when they leave that meeting, they are going to treat their teams the same way, with the same result from the teams. Eventually morale dies and with it so does any chance at crushing goals and achieving great results. Your best team members will leave, and your team and company will suffer.

As a leader, fear is not your friend.

Take Action:

The next time you want to let loose and fly off the handle, take a breath and remember this book. Try staying calm, identify the problem, talk about why it isn't acceptable, and create an action plan to fix it. See how your team responds.

19. Crazy Scary Goals

Iowa, 2015

I had been a product manager for John Deere for over a year. This meant I was in charge of the marketing efforts, dealer training, and new product offerings for the Round Baler product line. We had a stretch goal of 50% market share and I was committed to achieving it.

My last few years in the Army relied heavily on data analysis. From looking at IED trends in Iraq to working worldwide countering weapons of mass destruction activity, I had been trained on looking through mounds of information, finding out what was relevant, and then building action plans based on the data. It was a valuable skill, and as a marketing product manager, I tapped into that experience to figure out how we could achieve our stretch goal.

I figured out that the round baler market was heavily segmented, more than we had previously expected. While the initial assessments were correct that there were four different baler markets, inside of each of those markets there were additional segments. While John Deere dominated in the larger balers, our competitors had a stranglehold in the low cost options. I approached my supervisor to let him know that there was an opportunity in the marketplace for a low-cost baler option with certain features. "We've looked at that before, but the numbers simply don't work."

The competitive edge that John Deere had was a commitment to quality that outpaced much of the competition. In order to ensure the highest quality product, a rigorous testing regimen was implemented with every new product program. This meant that most new product programs required millions of dollars and several years to complete. A value product with small margins and relatively low volume simply could not pay for this kind of program, the return just wasn't there.

I was committed to getting this accomplished, and I was convinced that if our competition could do it, then we should be able to find a way as well. I set out on a journey to deeply understand our customer needs to figure out exactly what product our customers needed. I already traveled all over the country going to farm shows and testing other products, so I tacked on the responsibility of finding out about our value customers. After a few months of meeting with farmers, talking to dealers, and looking closely at competitor machines, I had a good idea of what the customer was actually looking for. I also took the time to talk to our design engineers who had extensive experience with the product in order to better understand the scope of the project.

I presented my findings and requested permission to build a team and start the process of building a business case to get the funding for the program. In order to make this happen, we would have to reinvent our methodology while still working within the constraints of our well-established processes. The key to making this happen was to build a winning team of like-minded go-getters who wanted to take on a new challenge and do something that had never been done before.

I brought in the lead engineer on the project first. He was a senior engineer with dozens of patents and knew the processes like the back of his hand. He was an excellent leader and a creative thinker that believed in the project and was a true asset. He was also a small farmer himself and deeply understood the customer needs and pain points.

Together we took a round baler and the list of parts to a small area designed for new product testing in the factory. We started ripping off parts and pieces that we didn't need, while also adding in the parts we did need. We knew exactly how many dollars we needed to take out of cost and developed several creative options that would meet the customer needs and also our cost requirements.

Our first team meeting was an interesting one. I presented the plan, how we were going to achieve it, and what our end goals were. Most were skeptical it could even be done, especially since we only had one year to do it in order to control our costs. I established a collaborative environment from the start. Each team member was not only allowed, but encouraged to bring up every issue we would face. We then discussed possible solutions as a group and left the meeting with a mound of action items to accomplish by the next week.

This type of discussion is extremely valuable in your team meetings. First, allow people to bring up issues. Then discuss how they may be solved. Make sure to press on your team that they should offer up a way to overcome the problem. Then, do not forget to list out action items from the discussion. At the end of the meeting you should remind the group of all the action items, who is tasked with what, and when that task is due. You should also follow up with individual, one on one, face to face discussions, especially when people are apprehensive about accomplishing a task. One thing I always tell my team members is, "Don't tell me what you *think* I want to hear, tell me the unadulterated truth." If you create a safe environment, and keep your calm, you will start to find real issues and creative solutions to those problems.

Once we had our team in place, and a tentative timeline for execution, we had to ensure that our plan was not going to interfere with the other product programs going on in the factory. The lead engineer and I sat down with the manufacturing engineering team in a small group setting to show them our plan. We discovered that our test build was falling right on top of another major program. Not only that, but because the other program was so large, most of our support team was going to be busy with this other program and unable to work with us.

"That means in order to do this, we need to go to market in eight months," I said as I looked at my lead engineer. The room got quiet, this seemed like an impossible task. "Can you do it," I asked the room of engineers. They stayed quiet and looked at each other, some of them looked down at their papers. Finally, the lead design engineer spoke up, "I can do it." The manufacturing engineer smiled, "I can too." The weld engineer looked at the other two, "Screw it, let's do it."

We came out of that meeting excited to take on this challenge, but although we had buy-in from some of the key players, there were other gate keepers we had to go through and difficult conversations ahead. One such interchange resulted when we started discussing the part development process. I'm not going to get into the details, but every part associated with the machine requires a process of part verification and then the digital background support network to ensure parts are ordered at the right time and brought to the right place on the factory floor. This is a very time-consuming process as I'm sure you can imagine.

"It's impossible, there's no way to do it." The engineer in charge of the part development process wasn't known for her collaborative attitude. I continued to press on her what we were planning and the measures we were going to take in order to get it done. "Unless you live in a perfect world where everything goes exactly to plan, you won't make it." She was looking to get me frazzled. In the past she had used this technique to frustrate people and get them into the anger state. This provided her the excuse from having to step outside of her comfort zone. I smiled, "ok, let's imagine a perfect world for a moment. What would I have to do in order to get this done?" She looked back at me skeptically. Not only did I keep my cool, but I opened up the opportunity for her to list all the issues she had and put the onus of execution on me instead of her. She went on to list a slew of problems and barriers that I would have to overcome. I didn't interrupt her, I didn't shoot her down, and I never got frustrated. For the next eight months, I made sure to always have the biggest possible smile on my face whenever I spoke with her.

In the end, we brought our product to market. It hit mature volumes in the first year and posted one of the highest returns of any project in the factory. We also put out a product that could finally compete in the value space. Our team was recognized by the CEO during a factory visit, and the VP made it a point to note how that kind of creativity was what our company needed to do to stay competitive in the marketplace. It was a huge win, and I am extremely proud to have had a chance to work with such creative, bold, and talented people willing to tackle a scary goal.

You're not going to get new results by doing the same things you have done in the past. If you want your teams to achieve new heights and accomplish scary goals, you need to create an environment that fosters creativity. People need to feel safe in bringing issues to light, and they need to be encouraged to come up with solutions. Your people are your greatest asset, and when you have the right environment that inspires and fosters creativity, you will see that asset come to its full potential.

In order to create that kind of environment, you need to ensure that ridicule is not tolerated, and you certainly cannot participate. What may seem like a ridiculous or a bad idea at first, with some thought and discussion, you may find that a version of the bad idea could be a game changer.

I'm reminded of the story of the invention of digital photography. Steven Sasson was a 24 year old engineer working for Kodak when he developed the first digital camera. The executives at Kodak had no interest in the product because it didn't fit with their current business model, nor did they have any indication that the market was interested in this product. In addition, the product would need nearly 20 years of technology refinement in order to compete with print photographs at the time. Kodak rejected the idea, and I don't need to tell you how that one turned out.

You also need to foster and encourage discussion in your groups. If your meetings are just hours of you listening to your own voice as you impart "wisdom" upon your subordinates, little will happen. You do not have a monopoly on good ideas. Often what I have seen is someone come up with an idea, and then the team builds on that to come up with something great. If your environment is one that does not encourage that type of discussion, you are basically shooting yourself in the foot.

Once you have an idea and a set of solutions, you need to work towards specific actions and tasks. Split up the solution into manageable chunks, then assign tasks to specific individuals with a clear time frame that is achievable and precise. At the end of every meeting make sure to go over every task, then as an added bonus, send out the meeting notes to all participants. This is particularly useful when people are late or absent, which will inevitably happen.

In order to disrupt the market and leap ahead of the competition, you have to find creative solutions. "The way we've always done it" is the fastest way to die. Change is a necessity, and the biggest driver of change is crazy scary goals and a team under the right leadership excited to take on the challenge.

For me it started with a crazy scary goal of 50% market share. Out of that was birthed the crazy scary goal of a new product program for less than $500,000 and eight months. From that came a series of smaller goals and creative solutions which resulted in a market disrupting product. With the right environment, and the right type of goals, you too can drive your teams to meet and surpass crazy scary goals.

Take Action:

In the corporate world, we often set goals on an annual timeline. Generally, that's driven from the annual reviews that most of us have. I want you to set one crazy goal for your team that may not be accomplishable in one year. Then break it down to parts that *can* be accomplished in a year. Get everyone on board and start working towards your crazy scary goal.

20. KISS- Keep It Simple, Stupid

A sk any military leader what the KISS principle is and they will immediately tell you Keep It Simple, Stupid. It's a planning principle that takes into account the rigors and fog of war. When you're getting shot at, it's extremely hard to keep a clear head and react appropriately to enemy contact. The more complicated a plan is, the less likely it is to succeed.

There was a senior manufacturing engineer when I worked at John Deere who loved to tell the story of a toothpaste factory. In this story the factory manager asked his manufacturing engineers to examine the problem they were having with empty toothpaste boxes getting shipped to customers. Apparently, the toothpaste tubes wouldn't make it into the box, and then empty toothpaste boxes would get packaged and shipped. In the game of a low price product like toothpaste, high volume and accuracy in that volume is the key to making money. Shipping out an empty box cost significant profit shortages and frustration on the part of their customers, and they were making this error several times a day.

The engineers decided to tackle this problem at the packout area. If they could identify the empty box before it made it onto the palette and shipped, they could eliminate the errors and save the company millions of dollars in lost revenue, costly shipping, and customer frustration. They eventually developed a sophisticated scale system that was able to identify the slightest changes in weight even as the conveyor moved at high speeds. When it noticed the change, the scale would set off an alarm and stop the conveyor. Then the worker nearby would go to the conveyor, find the empty box, take it off the conveyor, and then restart the line. The entire system cost nearly a million dollars but promised to completely eliminate the problem and would pay for itself in a year.

The first day kicked off exactly as planned. Within the first hour of production the alarm went off, the conveyor stopped, and the employee found the empty box without a tube of toothpaste in it. A few minutes later, the alarm went off again. So on it went, at least once an hour the alarm was going off, and the employee was going back and forth from the packaging area back to the conveyor pulling off empty boxes. The leaders were excited that the problem had been solved and were extremely satisfied with the implementation. Every time they heard the alarm go off, they knew they had solved the problem.

The second day started much like the first, the alarm going off frequently throughout the day. Not long after lunch, however, things seemed different. Several hours went by without a single alarm. Worried that something was wrong with the scale, they went out to the assembly line to investigate.

What they found was a shock and an embarrassing moment for the team of engineers that had worked for months on the solution to this problem. The employee at the packing area had grown frustrated with the constant alarms, so she took a large shop fan and placed it in front of the scale. The power of the fan was strong enough to blow away any empty boxes off the conveyor before they got to the scale! A simple $30 fan had solved the problem, and the lesson was cemented into the annals of manufacturing history: Keep It Simple, Stupid.

The other lesson that I took away from this story was the value of knowledge and information that your employees have about their particular job. I have nearly belabored this point, but you absolutely have to engage your employees and encourage them to come up with ideas. Whenever someone presents an issue, your first question should always be, "How would *you* solve it?"

This company hadn't placed enough value in the opinion of junior employees. The people that know the most about a job are the ones who are doing that job every day. When I was a program manager, I required my manufacturing engineers to sit down with the assemblers on the line to make sure the ideas for continuous improvement were presented to the people who do the job every day before implementation.

Iraq, 2008
Sometimes a simple fan isn't going to solve your problem, and a multi-stage plan is required to achieve success. As a planning officer in Iraq, I was once faced with such a problem. We were getting ready to redeploy back to the US and I was in charge of making the plan of transferring the battlespace to the incoming unit.

Typically, the RIP/TOA (Relief In Place/Transfer Of Authority) is the most dangerous part of a deployment. Outgoing soldiers are complacent and ready to go home. Incoming soldiers are unfamiliar with the terrain and enemy actions, so are less likely to notice when something is wrong. The enemy often recognizes the different unit and exploits the opportunity to attack. In addition, missions are usually running with mixed forces, so soldiers are in the battlespace with people they have never worked with before that might have different standard operating procedures, operate on different frequencies, and sometimes even have different equipment.

During my deployment to Afghanistan, a Special Forces soldier was killed just days before he was due to come home while supporting one of our units in a major firefight. Losing SFC Victor Cervantes was an emotionally jarring event for all of us, and it stuck with me for years. I wanted to ensure a smooth transition in a coordinated effort to keep the enemy at their heels and properly prepare the cavalry unit taking over our battlespace in southern Iraq.

Coordinating the movements of hundreds of troops on dozens of missions was no simple task. I had to find a way to make a comprehensive plan that coordinated our efforts but was simple enough for even the lowest private from both organizations to understand.

I got the team together and discussed the overall effort and the commander's intent from both organizations. Using the commander's intent as guidance, I delegated to each unit and organization to come up with a list of tasks and key missions that would need to be completed in order to properly handoff command. Once we had the task lists we worked on prioritizing them and then establishing a gradual transfer of authority from us to them.

The simplicity came in the presentation. I created a color coordinated spreadsheet that was set up in a hierarchical format. At the top was our command staff group. It showed how as the days passed, which unit would be in charge of each staff function of the organization. It also had a list of missions for every subordinate unit down to the platoon level and whether us or the incoming unit was going to be the lead on the mission.

The plan was extensive, and it covered weeks of missions over 100km of terrain. Every mission had a key task and element that needed to be accomplished and had supporting missions to ensure the safety of the soldiers from both units. We ramped up efforts and increased our presence to keep the enemy from capitalizing on the inexperience of the incoming unit. Eventually we were able to complete our RIP/TOA without a single successful enemy action during the entire event.

Because the mission itself was extensive, and simplifying the plan was limited, we were able to simplify the way we presented the plan so that every soldier understood what we were doing. In addition, the commander's intent, which was a short few sentences describing the goals and end state, served as the guiding authority for soldiers when situations seemed ambiguous. Through our efforts we were able to take what seemed like a complicated plan and simplify it so it was clearly understood.

If you are in an executive team, your company values and corporate strategy serve as the commander's intent. There are hundreds of websites and books out there on developing a strategy and values that are effective and achieve the same coordinated effort that you look for in your company. This strategy needs to be easy to understand and remember, and should outline the corporate goals for the year plus how you plan on achieving them. While many executive teams are able to understand this process, they miss on the opportunity to have subordinate leaders develop similar intent and strategy that feeds into the overall corporate strategy but remains focused and relevant to a particular team.

That being said, I've seen enough corporate strategy statements that are highly involved and detailed, asking every "commander" down the chain to do the exact same thing every year would be an exceedingly tedious and fruitless activity that would cost way too much money and effort. This is why the intent or strategy should be short, clear, and concise and have a plainly stated end state.

Say your overall company strategy for this year is to increase market share by a certain percentage, increase gross revenue, and increase the bottom line by the same amount. Each of your subordinate organizations will have different supporting strategies in order to accomplish those goals. Your sales team will have to develop a deep customer understanding to develop a plan to take sales from the competition. In order to grow gross revenue, you may have different divisions like parts or finance that can develop a strategy to increase their sales within the same market share. In order to grow the bottom line, your operations groups will have to develop methods to control costs (which requires leadership!) as will your supply management. Manufacturing teams will have to find ways to increase productivity. Marketing teams will have to find innovative strategies to advertise and bring new customers to the business. Each team has a different piece of the strategy.

In the army, the lowest commander that develops an intent is the company commander. Typical infantry companies are comprised of three to four platoons and about 130-140 soldiers. Think about your organization and how it is distributed in order to identify which of your groups would qualify for being "command level". Then challenge those teams to develop a strategy for their group that supports the overall company strategy. With a clearly defined intent, your employees can operate under a set of rules independently with room for flexibility in ambiguous situations, which continue to support the overall mission.

I'm also not a big fan of overly broad strategies, even though there are plenty of highly experienced people out there that will disagree with me (and many will make a good case). The problem is that the strategic vision doesn't tend to enumerate the actual goals behind it. For instance, "take care of our customers and place them first" is code for maintain current market share. Or if your goal is to increase market share, it means on top of the customers you already have. So I would say something like, "grow new customer market share by 1% while maintaining current customer base." That's a specific, clear, enumerated, simple goal that has plenty of flexibility for your subordinate units. It's a message that is understandable all the way down to the lowest level. It can be repeated easily, and everyone in your organization can mass their efforts in achieving that goal.

The point I'm trying to make is that simplicity is your friend, regardless of what level you are at. Whether you are the CEO of a fortune 100 company, or you run a small team of just a few people, apply the KISS principle and your people will have a plan that they can understand and execute.

Take Action:
Can everyone in your organization identify the most important elements of your strategy? If the answer is "no", then your strategy

is too complicated. If they can, do they know what their part is in it? Do they know how they support it? What are the top 1-2 things you want your organization to accomplish? Present those to your team, then during one on ones, ask them how they will support accomplishing those initiatives.

21. When and how to drive for success

At some point in your career as a leader, you are going to have to drive your teams to push out of their comfort zones towards a goal, even some that may not be that popular. If your stated goal is unpopular with the team, you need to make a decision about the amount of leadership capital you want to spend in achieving that goal. Every one of us has a limited amount of leadership capital. It's essentially a subjective measurement of the amount of clout you have within your team. Good leaders have more leadership capital and can ask their teams to do much more than bad leaders can (like climb a 10,000ft mountain against an enemy force that outnumbers them 4 to 1). I have always been careful about how I spend my leadership capital, and if I'm going to push and drive my team for a result, I ensure they fully understand why we're doing it and why it's important for every member of the team

Fort Bragg, 2006

When I returned from Afghanistan, I was moved to a different platoon. My second platoon was a heavy weapons platoon which meant they primarily operated out of light armored vehicles and brought massive firepower to the fight. Because the weapon systems were too heavy to carry by hand, the platoon was largely tied to their vehicles.

Within the first couple weeks, I took the platoon on a run. It wasn't particularly fast, but more than half of them couldn't keep up. When I took a look at their physical fitness tests, I noticed that this run was not an isolated issue; while they were excellent at maintaining their equipment and weapons, their fitness levels were lacking. I knew that in a few months, we would be deploying to Iraq, and after my experience walking during a firefight on Afghan mountaintops, I was unwilling to repeat that experience.

I gathered the platoon together for story time. I told them about our major firefight where we were out of breath. I told them about another platoon that got near ambushed and had to dismount their vehicles to assault through the enemy position. I told them about the squad who called themselves "billy goats" and how our foot patrols on restrictive terrain kept us from hitting a single IED during our entire deployment. Because of these experiences, I wanted to make sure they were all in the best possible shape to ensure when we got to Iraq that we would be able to take the fight to the enemy on foot if necessary. All the apprehension and gnashing of teeth went away. They finally understood my motivation for pushing them and were willing to work together to get better. They were also excited about the goal to have the highest physical fitness scores in the entire company and were ready to take the fight to the enemy.

When you execute the leader tools outlined in this book, you are going to have additional leadership capital to spend and push your team further than they have gone in the past. It's an amazing feeling when your team accomplishes these goals, and together you can celebrate these victories.

Some years later I was assigned to lead an intelligence analyst team working counter-WMD for a One-Star general's command. It was a relatively new unit that was stood up after the Iraq war invasion when we lost control of WMD material. The unit was comprised of Army, Navy, Marine, Air Force, and civilian personnel which added a layer of complexity to command and control.

A couple times a year the unit would deploy to Korea and set up a hasty command center to conduct simulated wartime operations. Before we deployed, I asked the sergeant in charge to gather everyone together and set up our mobile SCIF (Sensitive Compartmented Information Facility). The mobile SCIF allowed us to receive and transmit Top Secret intelligence information anywhere in the world. A few hours after I made the request, I went out to see our progress.

I had just come from the 82nd Airborne where we could make a phone call and within a few hours the entire unit could be assembled, with gear, ready to deploy anywhere in the world. I was disappointed to see that the container with the equipment still hadn't been emptied. The components had not been stored in a logical way, and several of the team members had never even set up the mobile SCIF before. We were just weeks away from our deployment and our gear was a total mess. I got to work with the team emptying the container and setting up the gear. After nearly 8 hours we still didn't have communications set up, but we needed to start tearing down the gear and putting it back into the container.

I gathered the team together and we discussed the importance of being proficient at setting up the mobile SCIF. If a national emergency ever occurred, we would need to be able to set up redundant communications quickly and make sure we had two teams in separate locations able to operate. This would ensure that any power outages or losses in communication would not hinder our ability to complete the mission. In addition, if we deployed somewhere, it was imperative that our facility be up and in operation as quickly as possible since all our soldiers would be relying on our information to stay safe.

We discussed as a group different things we could do to speed up our process. The team suggested we should pack our container in the order that we would need equipment. We could also split up the team, so some people would unpack, while others would set up. In addition, we all agreed that we needed to practice. I told the team that I wanted the intelligence section to be the first to be set up and running when we went to Korea. Since we were one of the smallest organizations, with the most amount of equipment, this seemed like a nearly impossible task; especially since we had just spent eight hours and still weren't ready. Once we had everything packed into the container, it was late, the sun was down, and the team was exhausted. "We'll do it again tomorrow," I let them know before we left.

The next morning, I had them all show up in their service uniform instead of physical fitness gear and we got to work before the sun had risen. I will admit that morale was not at its peak, but this time after eight hours we were set up and our communication was working. I congratulated the team for their efforts and the improvement, but it still felt like too long. Over the next few weeks, I asked the team to do the process again several more times. Each time they got faster. When we finally deployed, the SCIF was set up and running with communications within four hours. The team took a few minutes to catch their breath and sip some water, then in one of my proudest moments as a leader of that unit, they left the tent and started helping every other section set up.

A few months later an actual national emergency occurred that barely made the news headlines. We received the call around 4am with requests for information from some units overseas and a three letter agency. By the time the majority of the unit arrived at work at 7am, the intelligence section had our primary and secondary SCIF up and running, communications established, and we were busy answering requests for information. Our ability to respond quickly made the entire organization look amazing. The team was very proud of themselves, and they deserved every bit of praise that they got.

Over my career I have had the pleasure of leading tremendous teams that have accomplished great things. I was able to push them because I took the time to get to know them and saw potential even in the face of overwhelming odds. Every time the team accomplished an insurmountable goal, morale skyrocketed. In addition, the team started asking about the next crazy goal that they could set and smash. They welcomed the hard work and drive that they knew would be required in order to be great.

Take action:
What is one thing you could push your team to accomplish that may feel like a stretch? Maybe it's a safety goal, or a productivity goal.

Talk about it with your team and identify one thing that everyone can work on together to do. Keep track of your progress and find a reward that everyone can get excited about. Bring it up during one on ones and sidebar conversations. Make sure you keep positive reinforcement with the small victories towards your big goal, and when you make it, celebrate!

22. No Job is beneath you

There is something really special about being a leader in the Infantry. You are in the dirt alongside your soldiers, a victim to the weather, suffering the same exhaustion, hunger, and discomfort that they do. You learn that sometimes you need to go hungry so your soldiers can eat. Sometimes you need to take the midnight guard shift so they can sleep. Sometimes you need to give up a fresh set of socks. Sometimes you need to hand out your remaining ammunition. Always you need to serve them and place your needs last. This servant attitude is how you show with your actions that you value each and every one of them, something that will be necessary when you order them onto an objective under enemy fire.

I have talked in depth about having a servant attitude in your leadership. I can't stress enough how important it is in really setting you apart as a leader. If you really want to influence and move people to action, they need to know you will place them and their needs first. The challenge with servant leadership is that you must prove this through your actions and not your words.

When I was in Afghanistan, I rode in the lead vehicle. The prevailing military wisdom is that the leader of the patrol should not be in the lead truck. With the very real threat of IEDs (Improvised Explosive Device, or roadside bombs in layman's terms), the lead truck is typically the one that takes on the highest risk. By always being in front, I sent a signal to the team that I would not ask them to do something that I was not willing to do myself. I also carried my own radio, and extra ammunition on my back to pass out if needed.

The night we assaulted up the mountain, the enemy retreated back into Pakistan. We set ourselves in defensive positions on the mountaintop and waited for the enemy to regroup and assault our position. By this point, however, the enemy had a much better idea about the size of our unit, and it was clear we had massed a force of close to 100 Afghan and US soldiers on the hillside. My commander expected that the large force was a deterrent, and the enemy would not return with so many people on the mountain. He made the decision to pull back the majority of forces, leaving just my small element of nine men behind. The plan was that we would surprise the initial charge of the enemy, and the remaining forces would quickly respond, overwhelming the enemy.

We started camouflaging our positions and set in the ambush formation. Once we were set, the remaining forces made a large and loud display about retreating from the mountaintop. What you don't see in movies is the waiting that happens when you're in an ambush or a sniper position. After the first day with no enemy movement whatsoever, the men started to get restless. We realized that there was a good chance we could be up there for days, and we had assaulted with small three day packs.

Each man carried a few socks, a couple meals, some water, a poncho liner to sleep in, and extra ammunition. It had already been two days, and if we were going to last much longer, we needed to ration our food and water carefully. We gathered together all the remaining food that every man had and broke down the MREs (Meal Ready to Eat). We made a pile of food and started splitting up as equitably as possible. The sergeant in charge made sure that we split everything up with the soldiers as priority, I agreed with him. When it was all said and done, a single pound cake remained. I took it and crawled back into my firing position. I didn't make a big deal out of it, and I didn't tell anyone that I had about 300 calories to last for the duration of the mission. If my men were hungry, I would be hungrier.

We spent the next three days on our stomachs with half of the men on security and the other half resting, alternating every hour. I finally called the commander, we were out of food and water. The weather had also not cooperated, and it was hitting us with interchanging hail and rain. A small force of cold, wet, hungry, thirsty, and tired men was not going to be the most powerful interdiction force against an incoming hoard. We received a resupply of food and water on foot, and stayed a couple more days before finally pulling off the mountain; the enemy never returned.

While we didn't make much headway in our overall mission of enemy interdiction, we did make strides in building team cohesion and trust. If there had ever been any doubt that the leaders cared for their men, it too was eradicated on that mountaintop. The officer and sergeants went through the exact same pain as the men they were in charge of. We did not save the best food for ourselves, we did not exempt ourselves from the guard shifts, and we did not leave until every man was safe. We had already built great trust with the team, but after that week, our leadership capital increased exponentially. Any future orders to move on enemy positions, or take an additional risk, was trusted empirically and executed immediately by every member of the platoon. Our lethality increased, and not one single 3rd platoon soldier was injured by enemy action for the remaining eight months of deployment.

Putting myself in the shoes of my team members has always been a great way to show the team that I am willing to do anything that I ask them to do. Leaders exist to support their teams. Your main role as a leader is to remove roadblocks and difficulties; it's a servant position, you are not above them.

I was recently hired on a mid-sized company to be an operations manager. They have a special training program that puts candidates in different positions in all areas of the organization. I was on my third rotation delivering parts to technicians who only days prior reported directly to me. I did the job with a smile, and there were a lot of questions about this "lowly" position I was now filling. I made sure to tell them about the hard work and effort the warehouse employees put in every day to make sure the technicians were stocked with what they needed to do their job.

During one of these parts runs, I walked by two technicians who were talking. One of them had reported to me, the other was in a different organization. They stopped me to ask questions about the operations manager training program and when I mentioned that the training required me to spend time all over the organization, the employee who did not report to me spoke up. "Oh, well then you should come out to the wash rack!" I laughed. The wash rack was a messy job, in the elements, and there was no way to do it without getting wet and hit by splatters of muddy oil in your face.

My former employee got a huge smile in his face and excitedly interjected, "He has! AND ON A SATURDAY!" I was shocked that he knew. During my tenure as shop lead I had to schedule overtime on several Saturdays. Because I was a salaried employee, I didn't get paid for overtime, but as a leader I refused to ask my employees to come in and not come in with them. Since I was not a trained technician, I could not help them with their actual jobs, but there was plenty of other stuff I could do.

I set aside my regular business casual dress and put on the mechanic coveralls. I came in and did the dirty jobs: filling machines with grease, cleaning and sweeping, scrubbing down the mills, and running the wash rack. While I did it without fanfare, apparently word got out and the guys were watching what I had done. What struck me most was how proud my former employee was that his boss had done the dirty jobs.

There are few things that will motivate employees faster than a leader doing a dirty job. For instance, if you want people to clean, pick up a broom. The more senior you are, the greater the impact it is going to have. In addition, you will garner valuable insights and sometimes even find ways of improving performance and productivity because of your outside perspective.

Millions of people have watched the show "Undercover Boss". This is a show where senior executives of large companies go undercover in their organizations working the jobs of some of their lowest employees. This not only gives them valuable perspectives on the results of their policies, but it also gives them an opportunity to really get to know their employees. It's typically an emotional show, and nearly all the executives come out with valuable lessons learned from the experience. Many of them change policies and processes in response, and all of them gain tremendous respect from their employees for taking the servant leadership attitude.

You don't need a camera crew and TV show to do the same thing. You don't even need to go undercover. Simply make it a point to spend time working alongside your people and really get to know them. You will certainly find ways to improve the operation of your team or business and you will have the added bonus of increasing your leadership capital.

Take Action:

This week you need to serve someone. Whether it's helping them clean, giving up your parking spot, buying lunch for the team doesn't matter, but you need to go out of your way to serve the people on your team. Then you need to resolve to serve someone on your team every week. Soon it will become a habit which you can execute without thinking about it.

23. Failing to plan is planning to fail

The Army has a very structured planning process. Every mission has an Operation Order or OPORD that defines all the elements of the mission. Each OPORD has five paragraphs: Situation, Mission, Execution, Service and Support, and Command and Signal. The situation talks about what the enemy is doing, what they are most likely to do, what the most dangerous thing they could do, and it also tells everyone what other units are doing. The mission is usually a couple sentences with the who, what, where, when, and why. Execution is the "how" paragraph. Service and Support talks about the supplies that are needed and the support network to accomplish the mission. Finally, Command and Signal delineates the chain of command, and the frequencies that will be used. Obviously there's a lot more in there, and the higher your command is, the more annexes and supporting documents that are required, but every OPORD follows the same format.

This standard and methodology was very effective in helping planning teams consider not just the execution of a mission, but all the support network required to achieve mission success. I've noticed this is a major gap in civilian organizations. How many corporate strategies are accompanied by a detailed plan on how we will execute that strategy? Personally, I've never seen one. I've also never seen detailed plans that talk about the initiatives for the year that clearly delineate how each organization is going to support the overall mission.

What I have seen a lot of are functional area silos operating independently and rarely communicating with each other. Sometimes there is cross-functional collaboration towards a common objective, but typically organizations have their own goals sent down from their respective executive leaders that take priority over other tasks.

The nine principles of war are a set of governing guidelines for combat operations that can very well be applied to business:

Mass- Mass and synchronize your forces and effects on the enemy at a decisive time

Objective- Your forces should be directed towards the key objective

Offensive- Seize the initiative, then retain it. The best defense is a good offence.

Simplicity- I have an entire chapter on this!

Economy of Force- Use your forces in the most effective way possible towards the objective, the minimum essential force should be applied to ancillary efforts

Maneuver- Move your forces in response to the enemy in order to keep them at a disadvantage. Examples include using the terrain and weather to your advantage.

Unity of Command- Ensure all forces are operating under a single commander

Security- Prevent the enemy from getting an unexpected advantage

Surprise- Attack an enemy in a way they are not ready for

Take a look at companies that have disrupted and fundamentally changed the market, and you will see these principles in play. Amazon for instance, massed their efforts on a key objective, using economy of force: books. They took the offensive, had a simple plan, and surprised the competition. They answered customer needs and kept security as they grew, maintaining their foundational markets while exploring new ones. They maintained unity of command and unity of effort and have revolutionized our marketplace and economy.

In another example, Blockbuster video failed to maintain security and gave Redbox and Netflix an opportunity to outflank them. Both their major competitors acted according to the nine principles and bankrupted Blockbuster, once a powerhouse in their industry. Had blockbuster continued their offensive, they very easily could have developed a dvd delivery system like Netflix, or even rental and dropoff locations like Redbox. They got fat, happy, and complacent, and it cost them their business.

Put these two elements together and you can see how the nine principles feed into building a comprehensive plan of action that is clearly understood and executed in a coordinated manner. The five paragraph OPORD helps ensure the nine principles are being accounted for and acts as the framework to consistently consider all facets of the organization.

Now consider your organization, whether you are leading a small team or you're a CEO, are you giving detailed plans on new and important initiatives? Are you following the nine principles? Based on my experience, you're probably not. Instead, what I have seen are a series of small actions and factions operating under vague platitudes about "putting the customer first" and "beat the competition". I can pretty much guarantee that those strategic statements were hanging on the wall at Kodak, Toys R Us, and Blockbuster. I can also guarantee that you don't want to turn out like they did.

You probably already have key objectives and initiatives. Usually focused on Safety, Quality, Productivity, Customer Satisfaction, or some variance of these. You also probably have goals associated with each of these key performance indicators, so you're most of the way there in developing a commander's intent and end state. Now you can take the nine principles into account and start building a detailed plan that considers what you need to do, what your supporting network needs to do, and what the likely challenges you will face in executing that plan.

When I was the leader of a heavy machinery service shop, we would get audited on our contamination control procedures. Heavy equipment internal components are extremely sensitive to contaminants and the shop practices play a huge role in keeping equipment free of contamination and running at maximum productivity. The ratings were from zero to five stars, and my shop had been rated at two stars. As you can imagine, I wasn't happy with that rating at all and wanted to have a five star rated shop.

I created a plan of action and set my team into motion. We worked diligently, and I even got on my hands and knees a few times cleaning areas where dirt and dust would build up. As my team continued to exceed standards, I pushed my superiors to work with the supporting functions to make sure their areas were also meeting the same five star standards. Because of our fractured command structure, however, they were not in a position to give work direction to people who worked and operated inside our same facility.

When the audit finally came, my team got maximum points in every category, but because of a failure in a separate team, we fell just short of the five star rating and ended up with four stars. While I was extremely proud of my team and their execution, I was frustrated that our lack of unity of command, mass, and unity of effort towards a key objective prevented us from achieving our stated goal.

When teams work together towards a unified objective, the results are different. I deployed to Iraq as a planning officer. Our Battalion's mission was to secure the main highway from Kuwait to Baghdad called MSR Tampa. Tampa looks just like a highway you might find in the American southwest. Six lanes wide, it was built by Sadaam to ease the invasion of Kuwait. In 2007, we were using it to run supplies from the Gulf ports all throughout the Iraqi battlespace. Multiple convoys would travel across our area of operation which included more than 130 kilometers of highway.

Maintaining a presence across such a large expanse was impossible. In addition, we were in Shiite country, so the Iranian influence was strong, and they had imported their own especially lethal IED called an Explosively Formed Projectile or EFP. The EFP was about the size of a coffee can and it sent out a projectile that could penetrate our vehicle armor and resulted in a catastrophic kill inside the vehicle. They were also set off by an infrared sensor, so our attempts to jam communications would fail and the IED would still detonate. It was an advanced system that was easy to disguise and extremely lethal.

When we first arrived in country, we were encountering one of these IEDs about once a week, and while none of our soldiers had been killed, our luck was running out. We set out to make a plan that involved the entire battalion in a multi-pronged approach. We set up permanent outposts along Tampa in key areas of terrain. Each unit at the outpost was tasked with working closely with local police and tribes. We also started a Civil-Military Operations team whose job was to assess the needs of the local population and provide wells, schools, or electricity to meet their needs. Finally, we worked closely with our human intelligence teams and local special operations forces to gather information about key population centers and enemy supply routes.

Our methodology was aimed at denying the enemy the ability to maneuver in our area of operations and turn the population centers against them. Because of the coordinated approach of all these different units, all working together with the same objective, we were able to effectively deny the enemy the ability to operate anywhere the 82nd had control. IEDs along our route decreased more than 90%, and for the last couple months we were in country, we did not see a single IED event.

Your organization may likely survive without having to make a plan, but it can only thrive when everyone is working towards the same objective under a unified command with a clear and comprehensive plan.

Take Action:

By now you should have a multi-year crazy goal that you are working towards. You have set smaller goals to achieve the big one. Make a plan that everyone can understand and brief it to your team. Encourage them to poke holes in it and identify gaps. When you are done, you should have detailed action steps you're going to take.

24. Quick Hitters

The following topics don't necessarily merit their own chapters, but are still just as important aspects in leading your team.

Get buy-in from leaders formal and informal

Every team has formal leaders, but they also have informal leaders. These are the people that everyone respects and whose opinions carry more weight. For one reason or another, they may not be in a formal leadership position, but they carry significant clout. Watch your team interact and you will be able to identify who these informal leaders are. When an idea is presented, you will see people glance over at these informal leaders to see if they think it's a worthy idea. You may also notice that people nod their heads in agreement every time they talk. Sometimes it's a lot more obvious, and your formal leaders will tell you point blank who the really smart and experienced people are, it's likely they are also your informal leaders.

When you are planning on a new initiative in your team, take the time to meet with your leaders to bounce the idea off them. The first time your leaders hear about it should never be when you make it public. It is incredibly frustrating as a leader when you first hear about a new policy you need to implement at the same time as your employees. You haven't had time to internalize the idea and think about the methodology for execution. Inevitably your employees are going to ask for more details, and since you can't offer them, it degrades your standing with the team. In addition, it makes the leader who made the announcement look inept and takes away from their leadership capital.

I make it a point, when coming up with a new idea, to bring in my formal and informal leaders to discuss. After my presentation, I always follow up with, "tell me why this is a bad idea." I phrase things that way on purpose. The phrase, "any questions or comments?" does not actually encourage people to provide questions or comments. Culturally, it's used as a closing statement and people tend to avoid asking questions. You can prompt teams with a small adjustment like, "what questions do you have?" Personally, I prefer to ask where I went wrong because it's clear that I am looking for them to present issues. By identifying problems early, we can start collaborating on solutions.

Do first, then ask
I was leading a team that was frustrated that they were not getting the money and resources to improve their facility and productivity. These inconveniences didn't prevent them from being able to meet the established goals, but we were a peripheral facility and the flagship facility had all the latest tools and equipment which was driving much of the dismay among the employees. A new multi-million dollar facility had been built at the headquarters, but we

couldn't get money to add work bays to increase our capacity. At least once a month, during team meetings, the issue about our facility came up.

I challenged the team during one of these discussions, "Is that really preventing us from being able to meet our productivity goals? Is that keeping us from delivering machines on time? Is that keeping us from delivering on the expected quality?" The room stayed silent. Granted, the questions were mostly rhetorical, but they all knew that this was not preventing us from achieving the desired results as a team.

I offered up an example to the team, "When you want a raise, do you go to your boss and tell him that the only way you can do more work is if you get paid more, or do you do more work and *then* ask for a raise?" I have been in enough executive meetings to know that the overwhelming trend among teams is to ask for money with the promise of improvement. It's exceedingly rare for teams to present their improvements first, then ask for money to go further still. Teams that understand this principle and apply it are much more likely to get what they are asking for. Challenge your teams to execute and perform better with what they currently have, then use those results to request additional funding, facilities, and equipment.

Avoid the yes men
Let's face it, it feels good when people compliment you and confirm that your ideas are great. Drugs and Alcohol also feel great, but they are not good for you. The yes men will destroy your leadership capital the same way Heroin will destroy your body.

I'll say it again, you don't have a monopoly on good ideas. Sometimes your idea may be decent but needs refining. Sometimes your idea sucks, and you haven't realized the 2nd and 3rd order ramifications of your next initiative. If you don't surround yourself with people that will challenge you, all your ideas will go unchecked, which means your bad ideas will get out.

Every military officer has a senior enlisted member as his or her right hand. In the army every direct line leader from the 2nd Lieutenant all the way to the Commanding General of the Army has a senior enlisted member as his "battle buddy". These enlisted men came up through the ranks, starting as privates in basic training, and are often more connected with the plight of the soldier than the officer is. They understand the impacts decisions will have at the lowest level, and they are relied upon as a sounding board for ideas by the commanding officer. These are highly respected positions, and great officers will always confer with their enlisted leaders on major policy decisions.

As I have always told my subordinate leaders, "I already think I'm right, I don't need you to tell me that. I need you to tell me where this could go wrong." If one of my leaders never challenges a decision of mine or is unwilling to offer an idea that may run counter to something I want, I will make it clear in our one on ones that I need his input, not my input regurgitated back at me through him.

If you want all your ideas to be good ones, run them through a close group of leaders that will critically analyze them.

Give your opinion last
As a leader, especially in a senior level position, your opinion carries a significant amount of weight in your team. If you are being presented a project proposal, and give your opinion early, it is a quick way to shut down discussion (particularly in a large group

setting). If you carry a lot of leadership capital, team members will be less likely to offer a counter opinion once you have given yours. It is imperative that before you make a decision, you have considered not only the results of an action, but the effects that action will have across the organization. Staying quiet early on is an effective way to allow that discussion to build and the differing opinions to be presented.

I once watched a general receive a series of briefings from his subordinate and staff functions. Each presentation started with defining a problem, then presenting several courses of action. At the end of the brief, the expectation was that the general would make a decision. Imagine having the pressure of making a decision that is going to have large organizational impacts, many of which could literally be life and death, and you only had 30 minutes of information presented to you.

During several of these decision briefs, the general sat quietly and asked for input from his senior leaders. He also asked a lot of questions from the group, trying to pry out the issues that may not have been presented in the briefing. Then, once the discussion had satisfied his questioning, he would make a decision. Almost 90% of the time he came up with some sort of hybrid course of action that wasn't in the presentation.

Years later I was in a series of briefings to the John Deere CEO. I recognized the same trend that I had seen from that general. The CEO kept his personal opinion to himself, asked a series of questions, then asked for input from his president, VP, and other senior leaders. Finally, his opinion came last.

Both of these senior leaders understood clearly that when they made a recommendation, especially in a public setting, few if any people would be willing to counter them. When you are making decisions, you want to make sure that you have examined the 2nd and 3rd order effects of those decisions, which means you need input from the team. If you're not already doing it, start waiting and exercise some patience. Use questions and give your opinion last. The efficacy of your decisions will increase dramatically.

Have fun!
One of the surprising myths about leadership that I have seen repeated is that leaders must be stoic and that somehow equates to professionalism. This is highly unnecessary. It's ok to have fun, make jokes, and laugh alongside your employees. It doesn't degrade your standing at all, in fact, having a sense of humor makes you a much more likeable leader. In addition, taking the time and effort to recognize their victories with fun activities really builds the team cohesion.

When I was a program manager and my lightning team passed one of the major milestones of the project, I told my supervisor that I wanted to take the team to celebrate. She agreed that it was a milestone worth celebrating and proceeded to tell me the type of activity I should do. "They love to golf," she started, then continued with a detailed description of a team golf event she took her group on. It included the golf course, a schedule for the day, and a method for splitting people up into groups of four. All previous team celebrations were done the same way and I was skeptical that these events were actually improving team cohesion (which is the actual goal of team building events).

I had some conversations with members of the team and found out that most of them didn't like to golf at all, and previous events resulted in a few members getting sloppy drunk and obnoxious. The females in particular were uncomfortable with how these events played out and rarely enjoyed themselves. I set out to find a different way.

I found a company that would help set up a scavenger hunt in your local city. They had an app you could download that gave you a series of challenges like "thumb wrestle with a cop", or "take a picture with a frog", or "get a stranger to dance with you". Each challenge had a difficulty rating and a set of points associated with it. The app allowed you to see the progress other teams were making, upload photos and videos of the event, and eventually make a video or slideshow of the greatest hits of the group. This seemed like a perfect activity to challenge the team, have fun, and build team unity.

I had everyone meet in downtown Raleigh, NC the morning of the event. We split up into teams by functional area. This meant the design engineers, manufacturing engineers, supply management, marketing, etc. all worked together in their small groups. Each team had about four hours to complete as many challenges as possible, then we met at a local restaurant & Brewery for lunch and awards. I told everyone that I would buy them lunch and two drinks, anything beyond that, they were on their own. I also created personalized awards for every member of the team. It was just a simple certificate printed on cardstock, but it highlighted in a playful way either something they contributed to the team or one of my favorite things about them. The day was a huge hit!

It was awesome seeing the certificates posted on cubicle walls, and team members telling the stories of the crazy things they did or saw that day. Word got out in the factory and I had several people come and ask me about my future team building exercises. I also noticed that during team meetings, our activities that day came up. Not only did we grow closer as a team, but also other people in the factory *wanted* to be on my teams. It was clear we were high performing and we still made time to have fun.

I always welcome laughter, as long as it isn't at anyone's expense. Happy employees love to come to work and they are more productive when they are there. If you want people to do their best work, which you absolutely should, create an environment that allows and encourages laughter and fun. Your team will be more creative and productive, and best of all, other great employees will want to come and work for you.

Take Action:

This chapter is all about little actions you can take! Let's list them out once more:

1. Get buy-in from leaders, formal and informal
2. Do First, then ask
3. Avoid the yes men
4. Give your opinion last
5. Have fun!

Conclusion

There are no bad teams, only bad leaders. Throughout this book I have given you the necessary knowledge and tools to pursue real, positive, transformative change in your organization and provide the quality leadership your people need and want. There are simply too many bad leaders and not enough great leaders out there in the workplace. Whereas in the military there are centralized leadership schools, we have nothing of the sort in the civilian world, and it's difficult for organizations to make the right choice when it comes to training. I hope this book will serve as a primer in helping you identify what great leadership looks like.

Great leaders start by looking internally and leading themselves. They stay humble, act with integrity, and respect every member of their team. They are patient, fair, and have a winning attitude. They conquer their fear, using it as motivation to move forward. They know the little things matter and strive to be the best at everything they do.

212

Great leaders see themselves as servants to their teams. They understand that their employees must come first and will inconvenience themselves before they inconvenience anyone else. They value the input of others and work hard to promote and provide opportunities for all their employees. They spend time with every one of their direct reports in one on one conversations to ensure they meet personal and professional needs. They know their employees well.

Great leaders don't stop leading and mentoring people after they change jobs and organizations. You will often find them getting emails and phone calls from people that worked for them years ago but still go to them for advice. Great leaders care, not only for their people, but for their personal presentation, and the company they work for. Great leaders take great pride in everything they do.

Great leaders are not satisfied with "the way we've always done it" or "this is good enough". They have never arrived, they never stop, they always find a new challenge and push to it. They encourage innovation and creativity. They have fun and bring the best out of everyone around them. They talk about ideas and not people.

Great leaders bring positive change. They are an asset to your organization and will spearhead new initiatives and find creative solutions to your problems. They will increase morale, decrease turnover, and grow the bottom line.

Now the hard part begins. You've finished the book, and hopefully completed the actions. This is where it gets tough. There will be difficult days where your patience is tested. Days that everything seems to go wrong. Days when your work goes unappreciated.

Days where you feel alone, and you will start to revert back to poor behaviors. You get angry, lash out, exhibit little patience, or any other number of behaviors that you know you shouldn't be doing.

I challenge you then to take the time to self-trigger, have some discipline, and keep on leading yourself. Even though there are many of them, the bad days can't compete with the good ones.

Just as there are difficult days, there are immensely rewarding days as well. Days you get to celebrate with employees for a milestone achieved or a goal met. Days you get to congratulate and serve a new parent on your team. Days you get to see someone graduate, knowing you helped get them accepted. Days when someone looks you in the eye and says, "you changed my life."

Folks, those are the days that make every single minute of leadership worth it. Those are the days that you can hang your hat on and know that you left a great and positive footprint on this earth. You did your job and you kept on leading.

Afterward

He leaned his head back and rested it on the wood beam behind him, closed his eyes, and allowed his imagination take him home. He saw his son, a young boy taking his first steps. He saw his wife, the beautiful girl who he asked to be his girlfriend when he was just 13 years old. He knew then that he was going to spend the rest of his life with her. He smiled as he thought about the sound her high heels made as she walked down the street, it was something that always drove him crazy about her.

He took a deep breath of that hot Cuban air. As the humid musky breath filled his nose, he was instantly transported out of his imagination and back to the real world. He ran his hand across his brow, wiping off sweat and looking at the room around him and his team of fellow revolutionaries.

Rafael was part of a sabotage team that was going to support the Bay of Pigs invasion. They, along with hundreds of other anti-communists, had walked out of their jobs a few weeks prior in an effort to stall the economy and protest the latest government overreach. When his team heard of the invasion, they quickly moved to action and positioned themselves in the path that the retreating Cuban army would have to take.

They had trained for months on derailing trains, cutting power, destroying roads, and even working with explosives. They then took their materials and hid in the attic of a factory awaiting the invasion in a small, hot, room.

They could only step out at night, and even then for just a few moments. They lived in hot, smelly silence for months until the day their leader came in. "Gentlemen," his voice carried an air of disappointment, "the invasion has failed. Go home." Rafael stood up and asked, "what do you mean 'go home'? What about the revolution, what about freedom for Cuba?" The leader shook his head and spoke the words to the ground, "It's over. Go home."

Rafael had spent precious months in hiding as his young son was growing up. Over the next six years, he and his wife made it their mission to get their family out of Cuba and to the United States. Their home was taken away, they were not allowed to have jobs, and their kids were called worms at school and were not allowed to wear the uniform which singled them out as anti-communists. They sold homemade food, worked illegally, and stayed in contact with friends and family that had made it out earlier in the revolution.

When they made their intent to leave Cuba official, Rafael was forced into a work camp. He slept in a hammock and worked as long as there was daylight in Cuban fields under constant guard. The prisoners were fed very little and Rafael got terribly sick. He said it was the first time he thought he was going to die.

Eventually they made it out of Cuba, but now they had four children, no jobs, in a new country, without knowing English. Rafael found a community of other Cuban exiles and got to work as his wife Julia went back to school since her degrees were no longer valid in the US. He worked three jobs delivering bread, filling gas, delivering newspapers, anything he could find that didn't require him to know English and would pay for his time.

For years he slept only a few hours a night and worked six to seven days a week to provide for his family. He gave up any dreams he may have had and sacrificed them for his family. Rafael was a true servant leader who placed those dependent on him first, and through his hard work, he was able to make a life for his children here in the United States. He was my grandfather and I am so honored to have had the opportunity to learn about leadership from such a bold man.

In the fall of 2001, not long after the towers fell, he called me on my cell phone. Apparently, my mother told him that I was thinking about dropping out of college to join the military. "Mijo," his voice was somber and steady, "I hear you are thinking about dropping out of college?" I paused for a moment and responded, "Si Abuelo, this isn't really for me." He answered, "Hmm…let me tell you the story of how we came to America…"

He went on to give me the many details I had heard in the past; out of respect I never interrupted. Also, it's an awesome story that I always enjoyed hearing. He came to the end and asked, "Do you know why I was willing to do all that?" He didn't wait for me to answer, "So you wouldn't have to. So you would have opportunities. So all my children and grandchildren would live in a place where they were free to think and to grow. Now you have a responsibility. Finish your degree first, then you can go to war. You owe me that. Deal?"

My grandfather was the last in a line of people who I deeply cared about who were all giving me the same message. My best friend Chad Shields sat down with me for hours just a day or two prior talking me out of quitting, and now my Abuelito hit me with this heartfelt request. I don't remember if I agreed on the phone, but I honored the deal and I am so glad I did!

Between submitting this book to editors and getting published, I received a call from my mother to let me know Papi Tuto (it's what I called my grandfather) was in his final moments. He had end stage Congestive Heart Failure and Chronic Obstructive Pulmonary Disease. There was nothing left for the doctors to do.

I bought a flight that day from Tucson to Miami and arrived the following evening. He recognized me immediately and we spoke in between hugs and reunions with my very large Cuban family that had crowded into the small 100 square foot hospital room. I spent the next week alongside him and my grandmother watching as he drifted in and out of consciousness, cherishing the brief moments of lucidity, where we could talk before he would slip back to sleep.

I remembered his words to me, the story about how he escaped Cuba with his family, and now, in that hospital room, the plethora of visitors reminded us how he had positively affected their lives. "You owe that to me…" What could I possibly do with my life deserving of all that he sacrificed?

As I observed the different teams of nurses taking care of my grandfather, I decided that I wanted to honor him and his sacrifices and make a positive impact in this world. To that end, I have created Lessons On Leading, a training program designed specifically to create highly skilled servant leaders.

My program is designed to impart the lessons in this book on every leader inside an organization. I aim to create cohesive teams that lift up and support each other. Leaders that recognize the effort of team members and know how to support and motivate them every day.

My grandfather passed away on Easter Sunday 2019. The funeral home was so full that there were people outside that couldn't even come into the sanctuary. He was an incredible man that put himself and his desires last in order to put his loved ones first. I can think of no better way to honor his memory than by teaching millions of people the type of leadership he exhibited his entire life.

www.ingramcontent.com/pod-product-compliance
Lightning Source LLC
Chambersburg PA
CBHW030621220526
45463CB00004B/1369